This reader is graded to correspond with the Art~~~ ~~~

Artes Latinae
LATIN
SELF-TEACHING

Teacher's Guide, Lectiones Primae
Graded Reader, Level One

Waldo E. Sweet
and
Judith B. Moore

Bolchazy-Carducci Publishers, Inc.
(originally published by
Encyclopaedia Britannica Educational Corporation)

Consultant:

Grundy Steiner, Ph.D.
Northwestern University

Production:

Margaret L. Wood, Executive Editor
Judith N. Levi, Editor
Hedwig L. Jourdan, Production
David L. Dunn, Production Assistant
Larry D. Bloyd, Designer

General Credits:

John T. Davis   Helga Heaton
Marilyn McCarty   Thomas McCarty
John P. Nolan   Deborah Sweet
Elizabeth Sweet   Holly Sweet

Cover Illustration:
Detail of frieze from *Ara Pacis Augustae,* Rome

Bolchazy-Carducci Publishers, Inc.
1000 Brown Street
Wauconda, IL 60084 USA
http://www.bolchazy.com

International Standard Book Number:
Softbound 0-86516-297-2

Printed in the United States of America
2001
by United Graphics, Inc.

Bolchazy-Carducci Publishers, Inc.
1000 Brown Street
Wauconda, IL 60084 USA
http://www.bolchazy.com

TABLE OF CONTENTS

INTRODUCTION

The chief purpose of this reader, as explained in the student's Introduction, is to give students the fun of using the Latin they have learned. Without doubt, most teachers will wish to test their students occasionally on this material, but this should not be done so frequently that the reader seems like "extra work" instead of a reward for having learned the programmed text.

The most obvious use of the reader is for group reading in class. The number of readings in each Unit that should be covered in class is entirely up to the individual teacher. Some may wish to do only the first ten *sententiae*; others may wish to do only the connected readings. Some teachers have had great success with dividing the class into small homogeneous groups; here the teacher acts as a consultant, to answer students' questions.

The reader is also suitable for outside work. If the teacher wishes to keep the class together in the programmed text, an able student can do an enormous amount of individual work in the reader. The teacher will realize that no one would expect to have an entire class do all the readings. We have tried, however, to offer an almost inexhaustible supply of material to meet the needs of the entire range of student ability.

With programmed materials, an eager student may move ahead vertically as rapidly as he wants. With this reader, which is coordinated with the programmed text of *ARTĒS LATĪNAE*, there is an opportunity for extensive horizontal expansion as well. For example, while the class as a whole is working on Unit 24 of *Latin: Level One*, an individual student may turn to Unit 24 in *Lēctiōnēs Prīmae*, where he will find a Latin account of the gladiatorial games with Latin questions, 52 *sententiae*, and four poems.

1

Vocabulary

The experienced teacher will notice at once the large vocabulary of this reader. A word of explanation seems desirable. Whereas the programmed text purposely has a low vocabulary load, the reader aims to give students extra practice in the art of ascertaining the meaning of new words. This *skill* is what we are seeking, rather than the sheer accumulation of words.

Students should be shown how to guess the meaning of a word from the context or illustrations. They must learn how to make use of their knowledge of English derivatives. Here there will be a great spread in ability; to the student who knows the word "desiccate," *siccus* will offer no problem—but how many high school students know "desiccate"? The other side of the coin is that once they learn *siccus*, they will understand "desiccate." All students however, will be expected to guess the meaning of *horribilis*.

It is not expected that all derivatives will be known to the average high school student. If the English term is unfamiliar, the teacher may reverse the process and ask the student to figure from the Latin what the English derivative must mean.

Conclusions about vocabulary load based on studies of modern languages do not necessarily apply to Latin. We are teaching students to *recognize* the foreign word, not to *produce* it. The vocabulary "mesh" between Latin and English is very high. Students already know a great deal of Latin vocabulary; if they have studied French or Spanish, they will know even more.

New words in the reader are usually explained only once. There is no guarantee, however, that the student has read the particular sentence in which the word first appeared. He should work out the meaning as best he can and then, if necessary, check the word in the Vocabulary at the end of the reader.

While the readings in Unit 4 contain only structures already familiar to the student, some of the vocabulary will be new to him. The teacher may prefer to postpone these readings to

2

the stage at which this vocabulary appears in the programmed text. To take a few examples from Unit 4 of *Lēctiōnēs Prīmae: metuit* does not occur in the programmed text until Unit 6, *facit* until Unit 7, *lēx* until Unit 8, *indicat* until Unit 18. On the other hand, some teachers will prefer to do these readings just after Unit 4 of the programmed text, so that the experience may serve to reinforce later contact with these words.

A third alternative is to do only a few readings in a given Unit at first, and to return to the others at a later stage when students have met the vocabulary items in the programmed text. Considerable latitude is available to the teacher in this regard.

New Structures

It was thought advisable to introduce explanations in the reader for a few structures that will be unfamiliar to the students. In this way, more readings can be employed at an earlier date and the students can catch a glimpse of what lies ahead. The more advanced the class, the more the students can absorb this kind of experience.

Unexplained Structures

Certain structures are introduced without explanation simply as vocabulary items, particularly in the Additional Readings in the Teacher's Guide. An example is the sentence in Unit 7, *Nēmō sōlus satis sapit.* It is sufficient to tell the students that *satis* is an indeclinable word meaning "enough." An explanation would involve the fact that a) *satis* is an indeclinable adjective, b) it is here used as a noun, and c) it is in the accusative case used adverbially without a preposition.

Sources

Considerable care has been taken to check the sources of the readings. Wherever no concordance existed, locations have not been indicated; for example, in the programmed text, we did not verify the location of *Cōgitō: ergō sum* in Descartes, and therefore added a question mark. Absence of a question mark indicates that the quotation was verified.

An "adapted" quotation is one given in its common form, though not as the author originally wrote it. An adapted quotation is sometimes a misquotation of the original. An example in English might be "All that glitters is not gold" where the original is "All that glisters is not gold" (Shakespeare, *Merchant of Venice*), or "Water, water, everywhere, and not a drop to drink" where the original is "Water, water, everywhere, nor any drop to drink" (Coleridge, *The Ancient Mariner*). More often the quotation is transformed, for example, from indirect statement to direct.

In the case of biblical quotations, it was not practical to check the Latin since the author of the Latin version was usually unknown. In the same way, checking of the Latin translations of Greek authors was not usually possible. The biblical quotations were, however, checked in an English version for location. It should be made clear to the students that the Old Testament was originally written in Hebrew and the New Testament in Greek.

We have not thought it of sufficient interest to list most of the non-classical sources (medieval, Renaissance, modern). For example, all quotations from Burton's *Anatomy of Melancholy* are listed without location, and quotations from Othlonus are simply listed as medieval.

Connected Readings

The connected readings were all written by the author, although in many cases the story is based on an older Latin version. In writing about Horatius at the bridge, we followed Livy as closely as possible. Thanks are due to The University of Michigan Press for permission to adapt two stories, *Jūsta Dīvortiī Causa* and *Nāvis* which had appeared in *Experimental Materials, Book One* and also in *Elementary Latin: The Basic Structures* by Crawford et al.

Translations

We have tried to make the translations as literal as possible in order to reflect the structure. However, literal translation does not imply such a slavish reflection of the Latin that the result does not sound like English. When necessary, an explanation of poetical meaning has been supplied.

Explanations

We have tried to keep in mind the needs of the inexperienced teacher. Consequently we have often explained what will seem painfully obvious to one who has a thorough classical training. The teacher should also make use of the explanations given in the student's reader, since this information is not usually repeated in the Teacher's Guide.

UNIT 4*

Readings

1 One lawsuit creates another. (Anonymous)

2 Success feeds hope. (Anonymous)

3 Time diminishes grief. (Burton)

4 Necessity does not know any law. (St. Bernard?)

5 The cowl does not make the monk. (Medieval)

6 Trust creates more trust. (Anonymous)

7 God enriches. (Motto of Arizona)

8 Leadership proves the man. (Translation of Aristotle, *Ethics* 1.5)

9 Truth. (Motto of Harvard University)

10 The pencil (or style) reveals the man. (Anonymous)
You can tell what a man is by what he writes.

11 The Senate and the Roman People.
This was commonly abbreviated by the Romans to SPQR. Today the Italian government uses these same letters on some public works.

English Derivatives

Students should be encouraged to use the English derivatives that follow each set of readings. Knowledge of the relationship

*The Units of this reader are coordinated for use with the programmed text of the ARTES LATINAE program; for example, Unit 4 of the reader is designed to be used at the conclusion of Unit 4 of the programmed text.

between English and Latin has long been one of the acknowledged values of Latin study. Furthermore, the students can use their knowledge of English to help learn Latin vocabulary.

The capitalized part of each derivative given is the part that is derived from a Latin word in that Unit. Complete consistency was not possible. For example, we have written *PARent*, because the form in the text was *parit*. To have written *PAREnt*, thereby including the characteristic vowel *e*, would have been confusing. On the other hand, in *ALImentary* we did include the characteristic vowel *i* because the form that the students met was *alit*.

Additional Readings

Additional readings, similar to those in the student reader, will be provided at the end of each Unit in the Teacher's Guide. The teacher may use these for dictation, testing, etc. The beginning teacher is reminded that no class would possibly be expected to cover all the material in the reader nor this additional material in the Guide. We have tried to furnish the teacher with a virtually inexhaustible repertory to furnish variety and to accommodate the unusually talented student.

The Vocabulary at the end of *Lēctiōnēs Prīmae* includes the vocabulary of these additional readings, as well as that of the programmed text and the student's readings.

Diēs diem docet.
One day is the teacher of another. (Burton, *Anatomy of Melancholy*)
All subsequent Burton quotations will be from the same source.

Nēminem metuit innocēns.
The innocent person fears no one. (Medieval)

Diēs adimit aegritūdinem.
Time diminishes sickness. (Terence, *Heaut.* 3.1.13)

7

Vestis virum facit.
Clothes make the man. (Erasmus, *Adagia* 3.1.60)
   This is similar to Sentence 5 in this Unit of the student's
   reader. Since it is of some interest to students to see how
   various authors took a saying and varied it slightly, there
   will be many similar readings throughout the chapters.
   The students might be told that such examples of similar
   sayings could be multiplied many times.

Lūx et vēritās.
Light and truth. (Motto of Yale University)

Magistrātus indicat virum.
Office-holding reveals the man. (Anonymous)

UNIT 5

Readings

1 Injury destroys love. (Translation of Lucian, *Anth. Pal.,* p. 106)

2 Victory likes careful preparation. (Catullus, 62.16)
   The victory goes to the person who has made preparation.

3 Indignation creates poetry. (Juvenal, 1.79)

4 Innocence brings security. (Quintus Curtius?)

5 Experience teaches. (Tacitus, *Hist.* 1.5.6, adapted)

6 A beard does not make a philosopher. (Plutarch, *Disp. conv.* 7.6.3, translation)
   In ancient times a beard was a sign of a philosopher.

7 Opportunity makes a thief. (Medieval)
   If you tempt someone, he may yield and become a thief.

8 A drop hollows out the stone. (Ovid. *Ex P.* 4.10.5)
   In time even soft materials wear away hard.

9 The hour is fleeing. (Persius, 5.153)

10 Anger hinders the mind. (Cato, *Dist.* 2.4)

11 One donkey rubs another. (Anonymous)
   This is like *Manus manum lavat.*

12 The robber passes by the person who does not have much. (Seneca, *Ep.* 14.9)

9

The word *nūdus* means not only a person without clothes but also a person without other kinds of possessions, namely, a poor man.

13 The people rule. (Motto of Arkansas)

Additional Readings
(To be used at the discretion of the teacher)

Amor gignit amōrem.
Affection creates more affection. (Anonymous)

Volat aetās.
Youth flies. (Cicero, *Tusc.* 1.31.76)

Mūsicam docet amor.
Love teaches (people) music. (Translation of Greek proverb)
Someone in love will learn to sing and play in order to please the one he loves.

Ērudītiō et religiō.
Learning and religion. (Motto of Duke University)

Aemulātiō aemulātiōnem parit.
Competition creates competition. (Anonymous)

Teachers will vary greatly in the amount of time which they wish to spend in class working with the reader. It is suggested that the inexperienced teacher read a minimum of ten new *sententiae* in class in each Unit. Top students should be encouraged to do more by themselves or in small groups.

UNIT 6

Readings

1 Public affairs (or the State) teach a man. (Translation of Plutarch, source unknown)
   The State shapes the citizen.

2 Bitter fortune shows a friend. (Medieval)

3 Today the Circus holds all of Rome. (Juvenal, 11.195)

4 Always faithful. (Motto of U.S. Marine Corps)

5 Truth conquers. (Motto)

6 Willing and able. (Motto)

7 Brevity pleases. (Medieval)

8 The patient and brave man makes himself happy. (Publilius Syrus)
   The quotations from Publilius Syrus are not further identified, since in the standard editions they are listed in (roughly) alphabetical order.

9 Soft speech dispels anger. (Medieval)

10 Uncontrolled anger creates insanity. (Seneca, *Ep.* 18.14)

Additional Readings

Semper cōnstāns.
Always constant. (Motto of 51st Signal Corps)

11

Cōnsēnsus tollit errōrem.
Agreement removes mistakes. (Legal)

A person cannot be criticized for doing something if everyone has previously agreed on the action.

May we remind the beginning teacher again that no class can possibly cover all the material presented in the reader.

UNIT 7

Readings

1 Faith alone is sufficient. (Anonymous)

2 He fears his own shadow. (Quintus Cicero, *De Petit. Cons.* 2.9)

3 Every fox praises his own tail. (Anonymous)
Although *vulpēs* is feminine gender, it refers to foxes of either sex.

4 One flower does not make a garden. (Medieval)

5 Good clothes make even a stupid man appear noble. (Medieval)
Honestus has the idea of making someone appear to be a person who is deserving of honor. The English phrase might be "good clothes." This medieval type of rhyming verse (*stultum . . . virum*) is called a "Leonine."

6 Nature herself makes the wise man rich. (Anonymous)

7 Victory does not like rivalry. (Anonymous)
Victory does not go to the side whose leaders are in competition with one another.

8 Money alone rules. (Petronius, 14)

9 The miser is always in need. (Horace, *Ep.* 1.2.56)

10 Patience finally conquers great poverty. (Medieval)

11 Presence diminishes fame. (Claudian, 15.385)
"Familiarity breeds contempt."

13

12 His own deceit and his own fear trouble each person the most. (Anonymous)

> Adverbs are taken up in the programmed text in Unit 19, but will be introduced gradually in the readings.

The teacher should make use of the question-and-answer techniques which the students are learning in the programmed materials. A list of the different question words is given on page 23 of the Teacher's Manual for *Artēs Latīnae*.

Additional Readings

Ūna lēctiō nōn facit doctōrem.
One reading does not make a teacher. (Anonymous)

Fortis et fidēlis.
Brave and faithful. (Motto)

Nēmō sōlus satis sapit.
No one is wise enough by himself. (Plautus, *Mil.Gl.* 885)

> No single person is wise enough. *Satis* is the adverbial accusative of the indeclinable adjective *satis*, but this construction is similar enough to the English that students should have no difficulty.

Trahit sua quemque voluptās.
His own desires propel each person. (Vergil, *Ecl.* 2.65)

UNIT 8

Readings

1 One day begins something, one day finishes it. (Ausonius, *Id.* 14.40)

  There is a start and a finish to everything. You have to begin it on a certain day and finish it on a certain day.

2 The innocent defendant fears fortune and not the witness. (Publilius Syrus)

  Even though you are innocent, you may be convicted through some stroke of fortune; it is therefore luck, and not the testimony, that the innocent man fears.

3 The man adorns his position, and the position does not adorn the man. (Med.)

  We respect a man for what he is, not for the position he holds; we respect the position if it is held by a worthwhile man. An inferior man holding a superior position is looked down upon.

4 The absent love vanishes and the new love enters. (Ovid, *A.A.* 2.358)

5 The wolf changes his hair (skin) but not his mind. (Anon.)
  A variation of the quotation from Suetonius in Unit 15.

6 Where there is concord there is always victory. (Publilius Syrus)

7 Bad digestion, no happiness. (Anon.)

8 The letter kills but the spirit gives life. (*II Corinthians* 3.6)

  By following the letter of the law rather than its spirit, we are often destructive.

15

9 Bravely, faithfully, fortunately. (Motto)
   Or: with bravery, with faith, with good fortune.

10 Who can successfully conceal love? (Ovid, *Her.* 12.37)

11 God wills it. (Battle cry of First Crusade)

12 As bread feeds the stomach, so reading fills the mind.
   (Med.)

13 The timid person calls himself cautious, the miser calls
   himself thrifty. (Anon.)

14 The king rules but does not govern. (Legal; Zamoiski?
   1605)

15 An honor becomes an honorable person, but it brands one
   who is not honorable. (Publilius Syrus)
      Honors that are deserved are becoming; but undeserved
      honor is worse than no honor at all because it calls atten-
      tion to a person's defects.

16 Now brother deceives brother, daughter deceives mother,
   father deceives son, and friend deceives friend. (Med.)

17 Man proposes but God disposes. (Thomas a Kempis?)

18 The pig is teaching Minerva. (Cicero, *Acad.* 1.5)
      Supply the word *docet*. Minerva was the goddess of wis-
      dom, handicrafts, etc., and the pig (a symbol of stupidity)
      is trying to teach Minerva all these various skills.

19 Where liberty is, there is my country. (Anon.)

In *Latin: Level One* subordinate clauses are not introduced
until Unit 19. However, there are certain types of subordinate
clauses in Latin which are easy for a speaker of English because
English has a similar construction. In the reader, we have
introduced these in Sentence 6 of this Unit. The difficult subordinate clauses are those in which Latin omits certain items
essential in English.

Additional Readings

Virum bonum nātūra, nōn ōrdō, facit.
Nature, and not rank, makes a man good. (Publilius Syrus)

Medicus cūrat, nātūra sānat.
The doctor takes care and nature cures. (Anon.)

Christus vincit, Christus rēgnat, Christus imperat.
Christ conquers, Christ rules, Christ reigns. (Anon.)

Malus male cōgitat.
The evil person plans in an evil way. (Anon.)

Nōn est ratiō ubī vīs imperat.
There is no reason where violence is in charge. (Anon.)

Ubī dolor, ibī digitus.
Where there is pain, there the finger is. (Burton)
    Where we itch, we scratch.

Parva domus, magna quiēs.
A small house, plenty of rest (quiet). (Anon.)
    In small homes life proceeds smoothly; in large palaces
    things are troublesome. There is noise, confusion, and
    intrigue.

UNIT 9

Readings

1 One can recognize a donkey from his ear. (Anon.)

2 The snake is hiding in the grass. (Vergil, *E.* 3.93)

3 The palm not without dust. (Motto, based on Horace, *Ep.* 1.1.51)
   The palm branch is the symbol of victory; dust is the symbol of conflict either in battle or on the playing field. *Nōn sine* is an example of the figure of speech called "litotes." Therefore this motto means "Victory comes only with hard work."

4 The blind man is judging about the sun. (Anon.)
   He is making a judgment about something he is not competent to judge.

5 The prudent man lives carefully, the stupid man carelessly. (Med.)

6 Victory increases with harmony. (Motto)

7 No one sees when he is in love. (Propertius, 2.14.18)

8 My hope is in God. (Motto)

9 With virtue and work. (Motto)

10 With harmony, integrity, and industry. (Motto)

11 With constancy and virtue. (Motto)

12 There is never a good son from a bad father. (Anon.)

13 No rule without an exception. (Med.)
This can apply to the previous reading.

14 Prosperity from harmony. (Motto)

15 No day without a line. (Anonymous proverb about Apelles)
The meaning here is that success comes from unremitting
practice. Pliny says (in *N.H.*35.36.84) about this famous
Greek artist, "Apellī fuit aliōquī perpetua cōnsuētūdō
numquam tam occupātum diem agendī, ut nōn līneam
dūcendō exerceret artem, quod ab eō in prōverbium vēnit."
Apelles' industriousness passed into a proverb. It appears
in Erasmus (in *Adagia* 1.4.12) as "Nūllam hodiē līneam
dūxī."

Since Apelles was an artist, his "line" refers to drawing or
painting. However, the quotation is generally taken today
to refer to a line of writing.

16 Salvation lies in God alone. (Motto)

17 No one grieves for a long time except through his own
fault. (Anon.)

18 The flower in the picture does not exist, except just as a
picture. (Med.)

19 Just as fragile ice disappears, so anger disappears through
delay. (Ovid, *A.A.*1.374)

20 In love there is always sweet madness. (Publilius Syrus)

Additional Readings

Virtūte et labōre.
With courage and hard work. (Motto)

Maximus ē minimā scintillā prōvenit ignis.
The largest fire comes from the smallest spark. (Med.)

Sine jūstitiā nūlla lībertās.
No liberty without justice. (Anon.)

Labōre et honōre.
With hard work and honor. (Motto)

Ā Deō rēx, ā rēge lēx.
The king comes to us from God, and law comes to us from the
king. (Med.)
>   We should obey the law because it comes to us from the
>   king who in turn gets his authority from God. This is the
>   so-called "Divine Right" of kings.

In pulchrā veste sapiēns nōn vīvit honestē.
A wise man does not live honorably in fine clothes. (Med.)
>   A person can hardly be a wise man and spend much of
>   his time thinking about the kinds of clothes he is going
>   to wear.

Sine Cerere et Līberō frīget Venus.
Without food and drink, love grows cold. (Terence, *Eun.*4.6)
>   Without the necessities of life, even a fine romance will
>   fail.

>   *Cerēs* was the goddess of agriculture. *Līber* (the Liberator)
>   was another name for Bacchus, the god of wine. *Venus*
>   was the goddess of love. Here the names of the gods and
>   goddesses were used for the qualities they represented.

Deus ex māchinā.
The god from the machine. (Commonplace)
>   This refers to a technique in Greek tragedy whereby a
>   god appeared in a conveyance above the actors, thus often
>   resolving the difficulties into which the author had gotten
>   in working out his plot. The expression indicates some
>   kind of artificial intervention which solves an otherwise
>   insoluble problem.

The inexperienced teacher will discover that somewhere in the
next ten Units or so, the class will reach a "learning plateau."
To use another figure, the students will have reached a satura-
tion point. The place where this will occur is impossible to
predict because of the variables between classes, schools, and
teachers. But when it does occur, it would be wise to cease

20

work for a few days on the programmed course and use the other resources of the *Artēs Latīnae* program. In such a situation a teacher might conceivably wish to do *all* the readings for a certain Unit.

It is suggested that it might be well to have a short breathing space at the end of Unit 23, when the students have met the entire noun system but before they start the verb system. However, the individual teacher must be the judge of where and when to vary the pace.

UNIT 10

Readings

1 With faith and courage. (Motto)

Students may wonder about such constructions as *Fidē et fortitūdine*. The practice in Latin is to use *cum* in such expressions as "with fidelity" (*cum fidē*), unless it is modified by an adjective, in which case one may say *magnā cum fidē* or, omitting the *cum*, simply *magnā fidē*. The ablative without *cum* is also regularly used when there are two or more nouns in parallel construction, as in *Fidē et fortitūdine*.

2 With force and with courage. (Motto)

3 True knowledge with pure faith. (Motto of Beloit College)

4 Deception often lurks under a fair appearance. (Med.)

5 From the claw we can recognize the lion. (Anon.)

We do not have to see the whole lion once we see the claw.

6 Neither with hope nor with fear. (Motto)

We proceed neither foolishly optimistic nor in fearful fashion.

7 Deceit reigns in the lofty palace. (Seneca, *Phaedra* 982)

8 Where love is, there one's eye is. (Burton)

When a person is in love, he constantly looks at his loved one.

9 With courage and faith. (Motto)

10 A tree does not fall with (as a result of) one blow. (Med.)

11 Where things are prosperous, there is my homeland. (Anon.)
A person can travel from one country to another and feel
at home as long as his fortune is good. *Bene est* means "is
prosperous."

12 Between master and slave there is no friendship. (Curtius,
7.8.28)

13 Often the powerful man oppresses the just man as the raven-
ing wolf oppresses the lamb. (Anon.)

14 The lame man needs a cane, the blind man a guide, and the
poor man a friend. (Med.)
This is the first use of a verb taking anything as its complement except an accusative. *Eget*, like *caret*, takes its complement in the ablative case. Few verbs do this. *Eget* and
caret both mean "lack." Words which have the same meaning sometimes by analogy take the same construction.

15 In one hand he holds a rock, in the other hand he is offering
bread. (Plautus, *Aul*.195)
When the dog gets near enough to reach for the bread, the
man is going to hit him with a rock. Often people are won
over by favors; as soon as their confidence is gained, these
gullible people are destroyed.

Additional Readings

Prō fidē, prō rēge.
For my faith and for my king. (Motto)

Caecus nōn jūdicat dē colōre.
The blind man does not judge about color. (Anon.)

Pelle sub agnīnā latitat mēns saepe lupīna.
Under the lamb's skin often a wolf's mind hides. (Med.)

Antīquā virtūte et fidē.
With old-fashioned courage and faith. (Motto)

23

Fidē et amōre.
With faith and love. (Motto of Marquess of Hertford)

Necessitās dat lēgem, nōn ipsa accipit.
Necessity dictates the law, but does not obey it. (Publilius
Syrus)
> In cases of necessity, the law must give way. For example,
> there is a law against breaking and entering a locked
> building; if, however, a person is lost in the mountains in
> a storm and comes upon a cabin which is locked, he is
> entitled to break in and seek shelter.

Dē parvō puerō fit saepe perītus homō.
Often an experienced man comes from a small boy. (Anon.)
> Sometimes even foolish little boys grow up to be wise men.

UNIT 11

Story

The Ungrateful Snake

The farmer is working in the field. Suddenly he ceases from his labor. Who does he see on the ground? Poor snake! He is almost dead from cold. The farmer is moved by pity. He picks up the cold snake from the ground and places him in the folds of his garment. Now the snake starts to get warm and recovers from his weakness. But the ungrateful snake, in payment for the kindness, bites the farmer. The poor man dies from the effect of the bite.

After each story are Latin questions. For the help of the beginning teacher, the answers to these questions are given here in the Teacher's Guide. It is important to know that these answers do not pretend to represent all possible acceptable answers. While it is true that the question *Quem* will elicit an accusative of a personal noun, we cannot always predict what vocabulary item the student may choose. For example, in the story in this Unit the class may have decided to give the farmer a name, *Mārcus* perhaps. Therefore the answer to Question 3 might well be *Mārcum*. The teacher must be alert not to reject sensible answers merely because they are not the ones that he expected.

The teacher should use his discretion about whether to let the students refer to their texts in answering the questions. A procedure which has proved practical is to give the individual student his choice. The better students will respond to the challenge of answering without help from the original story.

Questions

1 Quis benīgnitātem ostendit? Agricola, homō īnfēlīx.
2 Ā quō anguis tollitur? Ab agricolā, ab homine īnfēlīcī.

25

3 Quem vīpera mordet? Agricolam, hominem īnfēlīcem.

4 Quō anguis dolet? Frīgiditāte.

5 Quem misericordia movet? Agricolam, hominem īnfēlīcem.

If the teacher wishes to ask additional questions but has not had the experience to do so, he is referred to the Teacher's Manual for *Artēs Latīnae*, particularly pages 9-10, 20-21, and 23-24.

Connected readings were not introduced earlier because of the difficulty of writing stories with limited structures. Furthermore the students feel a sense of accomplishment at reaching connected readings. For the teacher who wishes some sort of guideline, we would suggest that a minimum amount of work in the reader in class should now be the connected readings plus ten of the *sententiae*.

Beginning with this Unit, the number of English derivatives in the student reader has been reduced. The teacher may wish to supplement with additional derivatives; for example, *calēscit* and its connection with "calorie," *fābella* with "fable," etc.

Readings

1 Fire is not extinguished by fire. (Med.)
   If a person is trying to fall out of love, he does not accomplish this by seeing the loved one more and more.

2 Love and a cough are not concealed. (Anon.)

3 One day is pushed hard by another day. (Horace, *O.* 2.18.15)

4 Fire is nourished by wind, and it is also extinguished by wind. (Ovid, *Rem.Am.* 807)
   The same thing may have two opposite effects, depending on how it is used. Compare the story of the man who could blow hot and cold: hot to warm his hands, cold to cool his soup.

5 The crowd is not led by reason but by impulse. (Anon.)

6 A friend is proven in time of necessity. (Med.)

7 The cross stands while the world turns. (Motto of Carthusian monks)
The Christian faith is the one unchanging thing in a changing world.

8 Each and every tree is known from its own fruit. (*Matthew* 12.33)

9 A jug is never carried under one's coat for any honorable reason. (Med.)
If someone is walking around with a jug under his coat, it is because he is too stingy to share it.

10 No one is harmed except by himself. (Anon.)
No one else can do you any real harm. Others may cause you to lose money, etc., but true harm comes from your own behavior (cowardice, cruelty, laziness, aggressiveness).

11 The wise man remains as the sun; the foolish man changes as the moon. (Med.)
The moon is a common symbol of instability, because it waxes and wanes.

12 The poor man is honorably clad in old clothes. (Med.)
Poverty and poor clothes complement one another. It is foolish for a poor man to try to dress beyond his means.

Such observations as these offer an opportunity to comment on Roman and medieval views which might be considered snobbish by many people today.

13 Who is not wise after he has lost something? (Anon.)
"Locking the barn after the horse is stolen."

14 From smoke to the fire. (Ammianus Marcellinus, 1.14.11)
"Out of the frying pan into the fire."

15 Food is safely eaten at a narrow table. (Seneca, *Th*.451)
The adjective *tūtus* modifying *cibus* is best translated by an adverb.

If you eat at a small table, the food is safe; if you eat at a large table, namely that of a king or prince, then you may be in danger of poisoning. Because of the lack of adequate medical knowledge, cases of poisoning were hard to detect; whenever a person died under circumstances which were the slightest bit suspicious, poison was always considered.

16 Even in an enemy courage is praised. (Anon.)

17 A fox is not caught a second time in a noose. (Anon.)

Additional Readings

Ex facilī causā dominus mūtātur et aura.
A master and a breeze change for slight reasons. (Med.)

Emitur sōlā virtūte potestās.
Power is purchased by courage alone. (Claudian, 7.188)

Vetula vulpēs laqueō haud capitur.
An old fox is not caught by a noose. (Anon.)

Homō sānctus in sapientiā manet sīcut sōl, nam stultus sīcut lūna mūtātur.
A holy man remains in wisdom like the sun, for a stupid man changes like the moon. (*Ecclesiasticus* 20.32)

Prīma . . . crātēra ad sitim pertinet, secunda ad hilaritātem, tertia ad voluptātem, quārta ad īnsāniam.
The first mixing bowl goes for thirst, the second for gaiety, the third for pleasure, and the fourth for insanity. (Apuleius, *Fl.* 4.20)

    Sitis is one of the few words that has *-im* in the accusative singular. The meaning of *voluptās* here is probably sexual desire. The meaning is that a person has the first drink because he's thirsty, the second one leads him to gaiety, the third one impels him toward desire, and the fourth one drives him to acts of insanity. This is one of the readings which is more suitable for a mature group than for junior high students.

UNIT 12

Poem

This nursery rhyme will be familiar to most students. Here is the original. Because of the repetition, it is necessary to give only the last stanza.

On the Hill

And on the bird there was a feather;
Feather on the bird,
bird in the egg,
egg in the nest,
nest on the branch,
branch on the tree,
tree on the hill,
and the hill stood still.

In order to use the poem at this level, we have transformed the verbs in the Latin version to present tense. This is a good example of a reading where translation does not seem like a good technique, since many of the students presumably already know the original.

On the other hand, it lends itself well to question and answer. First is direct substitution; for example, *Quid in colle est?* and *Quō locō est quercus?* Then there is transformation: *Quid habet quercus? Rāmum habet.* Thus we may get all three cases of the noun: the nominative and the ablative by substitution, and the accusative by transformation.

The meter in this poem is an English one.

Questions

1 Quid habet quercum? Collis.
2 Quid habet rāmum? Quercus.

3 Quō locō est nīdus? In rāmō.
4 Quid in nīdō est? Ōvum.
5 Quid habet nīdus? Ōvum.
6 Quid in ōvō est? Avis.
7 Quō locō est avis? In ōvō.
8 Quō locō est quercus? In colle.
9 Quid habet avis? Pennam.
10 Quid nōn movētur? Collis.

Readings

1 Man plants, man waters, but God gives the increase. (Motto of Merchant Taylor's School)

2 Peace is created by war. (Nepos, *Epam.*5)

3 A great fire is often started from a small spark. (Anon.)

4 Evil is often sought, and good is often fled from. (Anon.)
Fugiō may be either intransitive, meaning "to flee," or transitive, meaning "to flee from."

5 Truth always exists in wine, in anger, and in a child. (Anon.)

6 Beauty perishes by wine, (and) by wine youth is destroyed. (Anon.)

7 Anger creates hatred, harmony nourishes love. (Dionysius Cato, 1.36)

8 The wise man corrects his own fault from the fault of someone else. (Publilius Syrus)

9 While a cat sleeps, the mouse rejoices and leaps from his hole. (Med.)
Antrum is a cavern or cave; it is a grandiose word to use for a mouse hole.

10 A woman smells right when she does not smell at all. (Plautus, *Most.*273)

11 For the public good. (Commonplace)

12 There is often wisdom under a dirty cloak. (Caecilius, from Cicero, *Tusc*.3.56)

13 Boldness increases through trial. (Pliny, *Ep*.9.33.6)

14 An old man rarely changes his mind. (Med.)

15 Enthusiasm creates enthusiasm, while laziness creates more laziness. (Anon.)

16 Only virtue furnishes joy that is perpetual and secure. (Seneca, *Ep*.27.3)

17 Marriage without offspring is like the day without the sun. (Anon.)

18 Food is eaten in safety at a narrow table,
   but poison is drunk out of golden cups. (Seneca, *Th*. 451-2)
   The first part of this quotation is from a reading in the last Unit; here the second line is added. This does not occur very often, but occasionally it seems of interest to introduce part of a quotation and then add to it.

19 Iron is sharpened by iron. (*Proverbs* 27.17)
   A person is stimulated by someone similar to himself.

20 The wolf turns his attention not toward his studies but toward the lamb. (Med.)

21 Anger quickly makes a stupid man out of a wise one. (Med.)
   An alternate construction would be to have *sapientem virum*, instead of *dē sapientī virō*, because *facit* can take two accusatives "to make somebody something." If there is danger of ambiguity, then the construction seen here can be used.

22 With courage and merit. (Motto)

23 Time flies. (Commonplace)

24 A wise man changes his proposal, but a stupid man clings to it. (Petrarch, *Ecl.* 8.12)

25 The gladiator makes up his mind in the arena. (Seneca, *Ep.* 22.1)
"Don't cross your bridges until you come to them." The gladiator cannot decide in advance (except in general terms) what his fight plan is going to be.

26 The law punishes lying. (Legal)

27 Nature abhors a vacuum. (Spinoza, *Ethics*, part 1.15)

28 Every safety lies in steel. (Seneca, *H.F.* 347)
One's only hope lies in recourse to arms.

29 Truth creates hatred. (Burton)
People often find it hard to face the truth gracefully.

30 The result is in doubt. (Ovid, *M.* 12.522)

31 Heaven itself is sought through foolishness. (Burton)
Throughout antiquity, and indeed within the memory of living man, trying to fly was considered the ultimate in futile endeavors.

32 From the example of someone else's difficulties, the wise man changes and corrects himself. (Med.)

33 A weed grows quickly. (Anon.)

34 On a journey a witty companion is as good as a ride. (Publilius Syrus)

35 No one is unhappy except through his own fault. (Seneca, *Ep.* 70.15)

36 Your affairs are at stake when the wall nearest to you is on fire. (Horace, *Ep.* 1.18.84)

In Rome houses were generally built with a common wall. Thus, if your neighbor's side of the wall was on fire, you shared the concern. A further meaning is that we should be concerned with what is happening around us since it will affect us too. For example, a married couple, even though they themselves have no children, may well be interested in a good school system because it will make their town a better place in which to live.

Additional Readings

Tamquam in speculō.
As if in a mirror. (Cicero, *Pis.* 27.71)

Tandem vōx crēscit dum vīnō lingua madēscit.
Finally voices increase when tongues grow wet with wine. (Med.)
> Occasionally the translation of a sentence is improved by changing a Latin singular to an English plural.

In vīlī veste nēmō tractātur honestē.
No one is treated honorably if he is dressed in cheap clothes. (Med.)

Equus parātur ad bellum, sed ā Dominō victōria datur.
The horse is prepared for war, but victory is given by the Lord. (*Proverbs* 21.31)

Ignis suum calōrem etiam in ferrō tenet.
Fire holds its warmth even in iron. (Publilius Syrus)
> The meaning of this is obscure unless one understands the ancients' theory of the universe. Fire was considered one of the lightest and most unsubstantial of the elements, while earth (particularly metals like iron) was considered most solid and palpable. The meaning is that even the lightest of these elements has its influence upon the grossest.

UNIT 13

Story

The Fox in the Well

A fox is carelessly chasing a mouse and doesn't see the well.

The mouse jumps across the well safely.

The poor fox however falls into the well.

But help is at hand! The fox sees a bucket.

She puts herself into the lower bucket. But because of this action the lower bucket descends and the other bucket goes up.

The fox makes a great leap, but in vain.

Look! A dog is coming to the well. "What is in the well?" says the dog. "Many large fish," answers the fox.

The stupid animal puts himself in the top bucket and goes down into the well; the fox however goes up in the other bucket. In this way she escapes from the well.

Then the smart little fox laughs at the dog.

Questions

1 Quāle animal est vulpēs? Facile ("skillful"), sapiēns, ingrātum, nōn stultum.
   (The adjective is neuter to agree with *animal*. *Facilis vulpēs* is also acceptable.)
2 Quāle animal est canis? Stultum, nōn sapiēns.
3 Ā quō canis fallitur? Ā vulpe, ā vulpēculā.

4 Quantum saltum frūstrā facit vulpēcula in puteō? Magnum.
5 Ubī situla superior dēscendit, quid agit situla īnferior?
Ascendit.
6 Ubī situla īnferior ascendit, quid agit superior? Dēscendit.
7 Quō locō pōnit sē vulpēcula? In situlā īnferiōre, in situlā
alterā.
8 Quō locō pōnit sē canis stultus? In situlā superiōre.
9 Quis ex puteō ēvādit? Vulpēs, vulpēcula.
10 Quis in puteō sine spē manet? Canis.

Readings

1 Common danger creates concord. (Anon.)

2 The first digestion takes place in the mouth. (Anon.)
Food starts being broken down in the mouth before it
enters the stomach.

3 The bad vase does not get broken. (Anon.)
The people and things we care about are the ones that
suffer harm; the ones we do not care about are the ones
that remain safe.

4 Personality and not physical beauty makes a marriage
lasting. (Publilius Syrus)

5 Man always plans one thing, and Fortune plans something
else. (Publilius Syrus)

6 The old lady is dead, the burden has passed on. (Schopenhauer)
The variant forms of the perfect, *obiit and abiit,* are *obit*
and *abit.* It seems likely that what Schopenhauer intended,
if he actually did put this epitaph on his housekeeper's
grave, was the perfect, "The old lady has died, the burden
has departed." However, since the present tense in Latin
is frequently used in the historical sense, there seems to
be no difficulty involved.

7 As spring brings flowers, so study brings honors. (Med.)

8 One swallow does not make a spring. (Anon.)

9 There is poison in the tail. (Anon.)
Something that looks harmless may contain a hidden danger.

10 He is looking for water in the ocean. (Med.)

11 The hour finishes the day; the author finishes his work. (Conclusion of Christopher Marlowe's *Dr. Faustus*, written about 1588)

12 He acts like a sheep in his face but like a fox in his heart. (Med.)

13 There is no journey without an end. (Seneca, *Ep.* 77.13)

14 Man without religion is like a horse without a bridle. (Med.)

15 Cheap gift, cheap thanks. (Anon.)
If the gift isn't any good, the thanks for it won't be good either.

16 It is a true word: God breaks everything which is haughty. (Med.)

17 Nature never says one thing and wisdom something else. (Juvenal, 14.321)
The Stoics believed that to live well was to follow the dictates of nature.

18 There is no evil without some good. (Pliny the Elder, *N.H.* 27.32.8)

19 The fickle crowd always changes with its leader. (Med.)

20 Everything unknown is considered to be magnificent. (Tacitus, *A.* 30.13)

21 A poor man does nothing well. (Med.)

People do not approve a poor man's acts no matter what he does.

22 There is no stable rule in someone else's position. (Seneca, *H.F.* 348)
If you have occupied someone else's position unlawfully, it is a difficult position to maintain.

23 Where your treasure is, there is your heart also. (*Matthew* 6.21)

24 Nothing is rightly taught or learned without examples. (Columella, *R.R.* 11.1.4)

25 Kindly and courageously. (Motto)
The person acts tactfully, but also forcefully.

26 Sometimes the stable is repaired after serious loss. (Med.)
This is "locking the barn door after the horse is stolen."

27 Like rejoices in like. (Med.)

28 With courage and with divinity. (Motto)
By my own courage and by the help of God.

29 Nothing deters a good man from what is honorable.
(Apparently this is adapted from Seneca, *Ep.* 76.18: *Ab honestō nūllā rē dēterrēbitur* [*vir bonus*].)

30 Virtue grows powerful by wounds. (Motto)
When someone suffers a difficulty, it may spur him on to rise above it.

31 Either Caesar or nothing. (Motto of Caesar Borgia)

32 How unfortunate it is when planning is upset by chance! (Publilius Syrus)

33 No one is free from accusation of wrong-doing. (Anon.)
Or, no one is free from wrong-doing. The verb *caret* patterns with the ablative for its complement.

Additional Readings

Nēmō sine crīmine vīvit.
No one lives without wrongdoing. (Dionysus Cato, 1.5)
> This is ambiguous. The word *crīmen* means either accusation of wrongdoing or the wrongdoing itself. It means either that no one lives without doing something wrong or that no one lives without being accused of doing something wrong. In the context in which it occurs, it is impossible to tell which is meant; therefore we may assume that the poet meant both at once.

Intus et exterius ōrnat sapientia corpus.
Wisdom adorns the body inside and out. (Med.)

Saepe venit magnō faenore tardus amor.
Often a late love comes with heavy interest. (Propertius, 1.7.26)
> Love late in life frequently brings great rewards, like unused money which brings accumulated interest after many years. But in the context the poet clearly means that if you don't fall in love until you are middle-aged, Cupid will exact a heavy penalty.

Nōbilitās sine rē nōn est nisi nōmen ināne.
Nobility without money is nothing except an empty name. (Med.)

Omne animal . . . sē ipsum . . . dīligit.
Every living thing loves itself. (Cicero, *De Fin.*2.11.33)

Vīnum bonum laetificat cor hūmānum.
Good wine makes the human heart cheerful. (Med.)

Nūllum scelus ratiōnem habet.
No crime has any reason for it. (Livy, 28.28)

Summum jūs, summa injūria.
The highest law, the highest injury. (Cicero, *De.Off.*1.10)
> Sometimes the greatest injustice is done when the case is taken to the highest authority.

Nīl nisī cruce.
Nothing except by the cross. (Motto)
> Only through the Christian faith can anything be accomplished.

UNIT 14

Story

This story, based on one by Petrarch (1304-74), shows that only the stupid man listens to all advice.

Good Advice

A father, named Publius, and his son are leading their donkey to the city. The girls make fun of them. "How stupid these men are! Why do they lead the donkey? Why isn't one of them carried by the donkey?"

The father puts his son, Marcus, on the donkey and he himself walks in front.

Now these women blame them in turn. "That's a bad and lazy son. He is carried by the animal while the poor father walks with great difficulty!"

Publius takes his son down off the donkey and he himself climbs upon the long-eared animal. Marcus in turn walks in front.

They journey along cheerfully in this way. But another woman accuses them: "How exhausted with his work the boy is! The lazy father is carried by the donkey without any difficulty. Why does the father neglect his son in this way? Why isn't the poor little boy also carried?"

"That's good advice!" says the father. Marcus puts himself behind his father on the little donkey and with great happiness they proceed.

But this sight offends some other men. "Poor little animal! He is carrying an impossible burden. They could more easily carry their animal themselves!"

The joke is taken seriously. Father and son climb down and put the donkey on their shoulders.

Finally they come to a bridge where boys and girls are playing.

They are laughing and shouting. The donkey, frightened by the noise, frees himself from their shoulders, jumps into the river and perishes in a miserable fashion.

The story shows this: only the foolish person always takes advice.

Questions

1 Quod nōmen possidet pater? Pūblium.
2 Quod nōmen possidet fīlius? Mārcum.
3 Quod animal habent pater fīliusque? Asinum, asellum.
4 Quem ad locum dūcunt Pūblius et Mārcus asinum suum? Ad urbem.
5 Ubī Mārcus ambulat, ā quō vehitur pater? Ab asinō, ab asellō.
6 Quid vehunt humerīs suīs pater et fīlius? Asinum, asellum.
   (*Quid* is used rather than *Quem* since the questioner presumably does not know that it is an animal which is being carried.)
7 Ā quibus excitātus est asellus? Ā puerīs puellīsque.
8 In quem locum salit asinus? In flūmen, in aquam.
9 Quō locō perit asellus miser? In flūmine, in aquā.

Some of these questions anticipate the programmed materials. The students should try to guess the meaning of the unknown question phrases *quod nōmen, quod animal,* and *ā quibus.*

Readings

1 Every animal crowns its own children with praise. (Med.)

2 Compliance makes friends, the truth creates hatred. (Terence, *And.* 68)
   The word *obsequium* can mean loyal obedience or respect; sometimes, as here, it connotes fawning, like our word "obsequious."

3 The shipwrecked man is afraid even of quiet waters. (Ovid, *Ep. ex P.* 2.7.8)

4 Your face shows (counts) your years. (Juvenal, 6.199)

5 Prosperity has many friends. (Erasmus, *Adagia* 3.5.4)

6 Our personality lives in our eyes. (Pliny the Younger, *Ep.* 11.54.4)

7 When individuals commit it, murder is a crime; it is called a virtue when it is done publicly. (Cyprian?)

8 Few men, but good ones. (Commonplace)

9 In prosperous times many friends are counted. (Med.)

10 After the darkness comes light. (Anon.)

11 He is looking for water in the middle of water. (Ovid, *Am.* 2.2.43)

12 With faith and education. (Motto of St. Paul's School, London)

13 Literature does not earn bread. (Med.)

14 Many diseases are cured by abstinence. (Celsus?)

15 When a wise man conquers himself, he is conquered least of all. (Publilius Syrus)
> To conquer oneself is to liberate oneself.

16 Eyes begin a love affair, association brings it to fulfillment. (Publilius Syrus)
> You first fall in love because of someone's appearance; only when you get to know that person can the relationship turn into true love.

17 Bad crows, bad egg. (Anon.)
> Bad father, bad son.

18 The haughty person and the miser never are at rest. (Anon.)

19 The dead do not grieve. (Med.)
Therefore we should not grieve for the dead in undue measure.

20 The Fates come in fixed order. (Seneca, *H.F.* 190)
We cannot avoid fate; it is destined. *Parcae* is another name for *Fāta*.

21 The majority laughs at tears but has them within themselves. (Martial, 10.80.6)

22 Hunger recommends food; the hungry man despises nothing. (Anon.)

23 With a wise man riches are in servitude; with a stupid man, they are in control. (Seneca, *De Vit. Beat.* 26.1)

24 He is known from his companions. (Anon.)

25 Hunger makes (even) beans pleasant. (Anon.)

26 An unjust ruler also has bad slaves. (Med.)

27 Riches bring cares. (Med.)

28 Hard work nourishes noble minds. (Seneca, *Ep.* 31.4)
The Romans were snobs. The word *generōsus* means a person of good birth. People of good birth were obviously better than people of common birth. Therefore, the word means "excellent." *Labor* then does not mean manual labor, which the Romans abhorred, but rather, intellectual labor.

29 The first appearance deceives many people. (Phaedrus, 4.2.5)
Frōns is "forehead," then "face," then "expression"; *frōns prīma* means "the appearance which one first presents to somebody."

30 About the dead nothing except good. (Translation of Diogenes Laertius)

Don't say anything about the dead except something good.

31 They falsely call miserable slavery peace. (Tacitus, *Hist.* 4.17)

Additional Readings

Facit experientia cautōs.
Experience makes people cautious. (Anon.)

Vēritās et virtūs vincunt.
Truth and courage conquer. (Motto)

Ignis probat aurum, miseriae fortem probant.
Fire tests gold, misfortunes test a brave man. (Publilius Syrus)

Scintilla etiam exigua in tenebrīs micat.
Even a small spark shines in the darkness. (Anon.)

In Venere semper certant dolor et gaudium.
In love, sorrow and joy are always struggling with one another. (Publilius Syrus)

Cōnsiliō et animīs.
With planning and enthusiasm. (Motto of St. Paul's School, London)

Nec plēnō flūmine cernit aquās.
He does not see water in the middle of a full river. (Ovid, *Tr.* 5.4.10)

Nōn mare sentit aquās, nec sentit cōpia gazās.
The sea is not conscious of its waters, wealth is not conscious of its riches. (Med.)

Only people unaccustomed to wealth make a show of their riches. Or, the rich are unaware of the poverty which surrounds them.

Ubī sōlitūdinem faciunt, pācem appellant.
Where they create a wilderness, this they call peace. (Tacitus, *An.* 30.22)
> This refers to the Roman policy of devastating certain areas to create buffer zones.

Miserōs prūdentia prīma relinquit.
Prudence is the first thing which abandons unhappy people. (Ovid, *Ex P.* 4.12.47)

Nox et amor vīnumque nihil moderābile suādent.
Night and love and wine persuade (induce) nothing which is moderate. (Avid, *A.* 1.6.59)

UNIT 15

Story

The Small One Aids The Great

A lion is sleeping peacefully with his mouth open.

A mouse carelessly runs into the open mouth.

The lion aroused from its sleep closes its mouth.

Now the poor little mouse is caught in the lion's mouth. He sits on the lion's tongue, looks at the horrible teeth, and takes thought.

Then he walks and plans about his safety.

This walking around irritates the lion; he spits him out of his mouth. "Look! A delicious mouse! Mice please me particularly!"

The mouse vigorously begs for his life. With a laugh the lion lets his poor tiny captive go.

Not much later the lion is caught by hunters in a net and lies under the branches without hope. "Who will help me?[1] Where is my friend, the mighty elephant?"

The mouse hears this sad plea, runs to the lion and with his small sharp teeth gnaws through the net.

The lion thanks him heartily. Thus the small one aided the mighty one.

---

[1] The present tense in Latin is frequently used for an immediate future.

Questions

1 Quis in ōre leōnīnō clauditur? Mūs.
2 Ā quō leō irrītātur? Ā mūre.
  (Not "*Ambulātiōne.*" The question for that would have
  been, "*Quō leō irrītātur?*")
3 Ā quō mūs dīmittitur? Ā leōne.
4 Quī leōnem capiunt? Vēnātōrēs, virī, hominēs.
5 Quō vēnātōrēs praedam suam capiunt? Laqueō.
6 Quis leōnem adjuvat? Mūs, parvus, animal parvum.
7 Quid ā mūre rōditur? Laqueus.

Readings

1 The Indian elephant does not fear gnats. (Anon.)
  Elephās is a variant of *elephantus.*

2 In its activities nature does not make a sudden leap. (Lin-
naeus?)

3 It floats through waves and fire and does not sink. (Motto of
Paris)
  Paris has lived through many disasters.

4 The oak is thrown down by many blows. (Anon.)

5 God be with you and with thy spirit. (Ecclesiastical)
  In the Catholic church, the priest says the first half of the
  sentence in addressing the congregation, using the plural
  vōbīscum. The congregation replies to the priest with the
  second half of the sentence, using the singular *tuō.*

6 Praise nourishes the arts. (Seneca, *Ep.* 102.17)
  The word *ars* in Latin has a broad range of meaning. It can
  mean literature or education in general, as in the title, *Artēs
  Latīnae.*

7 Necessity makes even timid people brave. (Sallust, *Cat.* 58)

8 Fortune aids the bold and repels the timid. (Anon.)

9 Where there is honey, there are bees. (Anon.)
If you want honey, you may get stung.

10 The greatest stream increases from small springs.
(Med.)

11 The good shepherd gives his life for his sheep.
(*John* 10.11)

12 Talk increases where women gather. (Med.)

13 While men teach, they learn. (Seneca *Ep.* 7.8)

14 A period of time builds up cities, a single hour destroys them.
In a moment something becomes a cinder which for a long time
was a wood. (Seneca, *N.Q.* 3.27.2)

15 Punishment comes late on silent feet. (Tibullus, 1.5.9)
Although a person may not appear to be headed for punishment after wrongdoing, it will eventually catch up with him.

16 Fire tests gold, misfortune tests brave men. (Anon.)

17 Large fish are captured in large rivers. (Anon.)

18 Moderation in all things. (Platus, *Poen.* 238)

19 The fox changes his skin but not his habits. (Suetonius,
Vesp. 16)
Pilus is an individual hair. We would say "skin." The orig-
inal is in indirect statement.

20 Sometimes fear itself makes people brave. (Med.)

21 Sheep are not well taken care of in somebody else's stable.
(Med.)

22 The hours pass and the days and the months and the years,
and the past time never returns. (Cicero, *Cato Maj.* 69)
This is a good sentence for the students to ascertain the
meaning of the unknown words because they are in series.

Since they know *diēs*, they should be able to guess *hōrae*, *mēnsēs*, and *annī*.

23 Friendship either accepts equals or makes them equals. (Translation of Aristotle, *Ethic. Nicom.*)
You can't very well be friends with someone who feels superior to you or inferior to you. Either you consider each other as equals or you stop being friends.

24 They are men not in fact but only in name. (Anon.)
Quidem is an intensifier.

25 Death makes everyone equal. (Seneca, *Ep.* 91.16)

26 There are many trees, but not all of them bear fruit; there are many fruits, but not all of them are edible. (Petrus Alphonus, *Disc.* 22)
Frūctūs means fruit not only in the sense of apples, pears, etc., but of anything which is a yield.

27 The Roman state stands because of its ancient customs and men. (Ennius, *A.* 425)

28 Hard work brings about honors. (Med.)
Or, the reverse could be true, that honors bring about hard work; namely, if you are given honors, you usually have to work to justify them.

29 The blind see, the lame walk, the lepers are healed, the deaf hear, the dead rise, and the poor have the gospel preached unto them. (*Matthew* 11.5)
Here is another excellent chance for the students, because of the context and the parallelism, to guess the meaning of the unknown words. Once they start on the series, the meaning becomes obvious. For example, if the blind see, then who would hear? Deaf people.

30 Good laws arise from evil customs. (Macrobius, *Sat.* 3.17.10)
If people are doing the right thing naturally, then there is no need to pass legislation.

31 One night remains for us all. (Horace, *O.* 1.28.15)
Maneō, while usually an intransitive verb, may take an object, as here, with the meaning, "to wait for." Night is a symbol of death.

32 Even modest affairs (farms, fortunes, etc.) prosper with harmony. (Sallust, *J.* 10)

33 After death comes true honor and true glory. (Med.)
It is only after a person dies that we can really appreciate his worth.

34 Right overcomes might. (Anon.)

35 Abuse does not take away the right to use. (Legal)
If someone abuses a privilege, that privilege is not then removed for other people merely because one person has abused it.

36 They are lions in times of peace and deer in battle. (Tertullian, *Coro. Mil.* 1)
They talk big, but when the fighting starts they are timid.

37 Arts, science, truth. (Motto of The University of Michigan)

38 Flame tests gold, temptation tests just men. (Anon.)

39 Often one dog takes a bone away from two dogs.
(Med.)

40 All are safe where one person is defended. (Publilius Syrus)

41 With claws and beak. (Anon.)
With might and main; according to the weapons one has.

42 Women live under a harsh law. (Plautus, *Merc.* 817)

43 Evil communications corrupt good manners.
(Tertullian?)

44 Where wealth is, there friends are. (Anon.)

Additional Readings

Omnēs nātūra parit līberōs.
Nature creates everybody free. (Anon.)

Fortēs adjuvat ipsa Venus.
Venus herself aids the brave. (Tibullus, 1.2.16)
> If the students note the resemblance of this to the Basic Sentence *Fortēs Fortūna adjuvat* in *Latin: Level One,* the teacher should point out that the Romans liked to take a well-known quotation and adapt it to their own purposes.

Absentēs habentur prō mortuīs.
Absent people are considered as if they were dead. (Med.)
> This is similar to our law which declares that people who have been missing for seven years are, for legal purposes, dead.

Dīvitiās fortūna, studium parit honōrēs.
Fortune creates riches while study brings about honors. (Anon.)

Quid lēgēs sine mōribus vānae prōficiunt?
What good are empty laws without good morals? (Horace, O. 3.24.36)

Virtūs nōbilitat hominēs, sapientia dītat.
Virtue ennobles men, wisdom makes them rich. (Med.)
> True nobility consists of virtue and true wealth consists of wisdom.

Frūctibus ipsa suīs quaevīs cognōscitur arbor.
Every tree is known by its own fruit. (Med.)

Exeunt omnēs.
Everyone departs. (Stage direction for actors)

UNIT 16

History

Roman history can scarcely be called history before 290 B.C., because the records before that time were destroyed during the sack of Rome by the Gauls.

Horatius Defends the Bridge

The Roman farmers are working in their fields. But what is now appearing on that hill? "It is an Etruscan army!" "Who is leading them?" "It is Porsenna, the Etruscan king. But who is riding with Porsenna on the black horse?" "Alas! It is Tarquin the Proud! He is unjustly seeking his kingdom." Because the enemy is at hand, all the farmers move from their fields into the city; they defend the city with their soldiers. But the Tiber River particularly defends them. Over this river there is a bridge.

But this bridge gives a passageway for the enemy. Some Romans therefore begin to cut down the bridge with blows; others burn it with fire. But now the Etruscan army is[1] running quickly toward the bridge with cruel Tarquin. Publius Horatius Cocles sees the danger. ("*Cocles*" means "having one eye.") The terrified Romans cease their labors. But Horatius recalls them to their duty. "Cut down the bridge!" he says. "I will hold up the enemy on the bridge itself."

First he prays to the gods; then he takes his arms and places himself in the first access of the bridge against the whole army.

Such bravery astonishes the enemy. Then they make an attack on Horatius. He stands in the narrow entrance to the bridge and

---

[1] *Exercitus* is singular and the verb *currunt* is plural; this is called "agreement according to sense," since the army, although grammatically singular, is made up of people.

only a few make an attack on him at the same time. But he is in very great danger. Two other Romans, Spurius Larcius and Titus Herminius by name, run to his aid. Spurius stands on the right side and Herminius on the left.

These three brave men sustain all the attacks. Now other Romans are completing their task. They call the three soldiers to them. A small part of the bridge remains. Larcius and Herminius retreat; Horatius stands alone; he calls the Etruscans to battle one by one. "Fight, you cowardly Etruscans!" he shouts. Again the enemy is astonished at his bravery. They all stand without moving with mouths open, saying "He is crazy! He is challenging our whole army to battle!"

Then shame moves the battle line, and with a loud shout they throw their weapons from all sides against the solitary enemy. These stick in his shield, but Horatius still holds the bridge with brave stance. Simultaneously the bridge falls and the Romans shout, "Now our brave Horatius is dying!"

Cocles prays to the god of the Tiber River, "Receive these arms and this soldier," and flings himself into the river. Although many weapons fall around him, he swims back across the river to his own people without hurt.

The story is found in Livy (2.10), where Livy adds that this feat is better known than believed. It is not quite clear whether he himself finds it difficult to accept that a man could swim across the Tiber fully clad in armor or whether he is cynically observing that the Romans of his day would not believe that a man could be so brave as to do what Horatius did.

If the students wish to know how Horatius could make the prayer when the bridge had fallen, point out that it was a wooden bridge and would therefore have at least a part remaining out of water.

The students will be glad to know that as the story goes, the grateful citizens put up a statue of Horatius and gave him as much land as he could plow a furrow around in a single day. Furthermore, each and every citizen, even in this time of lack

of food, contributed from his own store of provisions to
Horatius in gratitude.

The teacher might enjoy reading to the class the same story in
Macaulay's *Lays of Ancient Rome.*

Since this story is considerably longer than the ones which the
students have met before, it may be necessary to reduce the
number of *sententiae* read in class.

Questions

1 Quālis rēx est Tarquinius Superbus? Crūdēlis, injūstus.
2 Quōs Tiberis flūmen adjuvat? Rōmānōs.
   (*"Eōs"* is definitely wrong. It would be the same as answering "Them" in English to the question, "Who does the
   Tiber protect?")
3 Quis in ponte sōlus stat? Horātius.
4 Quod nōmen sīgnificat "habēns ūnum oculum?" Cocles.
5 Quī in Horātium impetum faciunt? Etruscī mīlitēs, hostēs.
6 Quibuscum Horātius pontem contrā Etruscum exercitum
   dēfendit? Cum mīlitibus Rōmānīs, cum Spuriō Larciō et
   Titō Herminiō.
7 Quibus rēbus pōns ā Rōmānīs frangitur? Igne et ictibus.
8 Quī Horātium fortem adjuvant? Amīcī, Spurius Larcius et
Titus Herminius.
   (Very few students will be able to produce the names of
   Horatius' two companions without referring to the text.)
9 Quid jaciunt Etruscī in Horātium? Tēla.
10 Quem in locum salit Horātius? In flūmen, in Tiberim, in
aquam.

Readings

At about this point the different abilities of the students will
become more apparent. There are two courses open for the good
student. He may be permitted to move ahead in the program or
he can expand laterally by doing more of these readings than
the average student. The beginning teacher may well be astonished at the amount of work these students will do if permitted

to proceed on their own. Students of this kind rarely need to have their work checked, and can go to each other for assistance, leaving the teacher free to concentrate on the students who cannot work profitably by themselves.

1 Does Diana on high care about the barking dog? (Anon.)
This refers to Diana in her role as goddess of the moon, who pays no attention to the dog barking below.

2 Wicked poisons lie under sweet honey. (Ovid, *Am.* 1.8.104)
Things which appear to be pleasant are often very dangerous.

3 Many courses bring many diseases. (Pliny, *N.H.* 11.52)
The formal Roman dinner (*cēna*) consisted of a *gustātiō* (something like our hors d'oeuvres, including eggs, lettuce, etc.), then the *cēna* (meat, fish, etc.), and finally the *secunda mēnsa* (oftentimes fruit). However, more luxurious Romans broke the *cēna* into many courses. Pliny's advice is to avoid over-eating.

4 The people judge a few things by their truth, and many by their opinion. (Cicero, *Q. Ros. Com.* 10)

5 Labor conquers all things. (Vergil, *G.* 1.145)
This is an echo of the saying *"Amor omnia vincit."*

6 Jupiter rules everything in the sky, Caesar rules everything on earth. (Anon. author in *Carmina Vergiliana* from *Poetae Latinae Minores*, Vol. 4, p. 160)
Somewhat the same thought as expressed in the Bible: "Render unto Caesar the things that are Caesar's."

7 The law does not care about trifles. (Legal)
A judge may throw a matter out of court if he feels that it is too trifling to take up the attention of the court.

8 A fox is not caught by gifts. (Med.)

9 When stupid people avoid faults, they run into the opposite faults. (Horace, *S.* 1.2.24)

10 The stars rule men, but God rules the stars. (Anon.)
This is a defense of astrology, saying that through a study of the stars, which are directed by God, we can know the will of God.

11 A flowing wave does not return; the rushing hour does not return. (Med.)

12 The stupid man is not corrected by words. (Med.)

13 Poetry does not bring bread. (Anon.)

14 In time of war the laws are silent. (Cicero, *Pro Mil.* 4.10)
Martial law is declared in time of war.

15 Many inconveniences surround an old man. (Anon.)

16 Few things but good ones. (Anon.)
This might be said of a modest household in which the furnishings were in good taste. *Paucī* would mean "few people."

17 Reason conquers all things. (Anon.)

18 Time changes everything. (Anon.)

19 Words move people, examples draw them on. (Anon.)
Our example, rather than our advice, will guide other people.

20 Deeds, not words. (Commonplace)

21 Exterior acts indicate interior secrets. (Legal; this is believed to have come from Coke)
We can guess a person's motives from the way he acts.

22 With courage, not words. (Motto)

23 Fire, sea, woman: three bad things. (Med.)
You can lose your property due to fire, shipwreck, or a woman.

56

24 Anger furnishes arms. (Vergil, *A.* 1.150)
   When a riot starts, weapons seem to appear by magic:
   clubs, knives, etc.

25 A faithful friend is recognized in adverse circumstances.
   (Anon.)

26 Through study and honest activities. (Motto)

27 With courage and arms. (Motto of Mississippi)

28 The stomach does not hear advice. (Seneca, *Ep.* 21.11)
   This idea is taken up again in the medieval quotation below
   (Reading 44): a hungry man needs to be fed first before
   he will listen to our ideas.

29 Mortal acts never fool the gods. (Ovid, *Tr.* 1.2.97)

30 With God helping. (Motto)

31 When two people are quarreling, the third gets the profit.
   (Med.)

32 With God willing. (Commonplace)
   Frequently used to qualify a statement, such as, "I will
   graduate in June, *Deō volente.*"

33 Peace is sought by savage arms. (Statius, *Theb.* 7.554)
   Through evil, good may result.

34 A person's speech shows his character and his inner personality. (Med.)

35 Often the greatest minds lie hidden. (Plautus, *Capt.* 165)
   Similar to the theme in Gray's "Elegy in a Country Church-
   yard," about the people who might have been Miltons and
   Cromwells but who were destined because of obscure
   origin to remain unknown.

36 When one dog barks, another dog immediately starts to
   bark. (Anon.)

When one person starts to criticize, then others will also criticize without having any reason.

37 Many types of hatred lie hidden under a pleasant expression and (even) under a kiss. (Med.)

38 Often a silent face has voice and words. (Ovid, *A.A.* 1.574)
A person does not necessarily need to speak in order to convey his feelings. In the British Army, a soldier may be convicted of "dumb insolence" when he has *said* nothing but has still indicated his contempt for his superior.

39 With God leading. (Commonplace)

40 Courage increases in dangerous circumstances. (Lucan, *Phars.* 3.604)
A person who is truly courageous will become more and not less brave as the danger increases.

41 Often, when one god is hostile, another god brings help. (Ovid, *Tr.* 1.2.4)

42 Like things are cured by like. (Samuel Hahnemann)
Motto of the School of Homeopathic Medicine, whose originator was Samuel Hahnemann. The theory was that diseases could be cured by giving people small doses of medicine which, in healthy persons, would produce symptoms similar to that of the disease. This theory was put forth about 1800 and enjoyed great popularity, but its influence has decreased since 1900.

43 Not every land brings forth all kinds of fruit. (Anon.)
Don't complain because you can't grow oranges in your yard.

44 A hungry stomach does not gladly listen to speeches. (Med.)

45 Somebody in all areas of endeavor, nobody in separate matters. (Burton)
Jack of all trades, master of none.

46 Every lover deceives the person he loves. (Ovid. *Rem. Am.* 95)

   Omnis amor means "every love affair" or, as we would say, "every lover."

47 Much, not many. (Pliny the Younger, *Ep.* 7.9)

   Quality, and not quantity.

48 Concerning this, many people know much, everybody knows something, and nobody knows enough. (Anon.)

49 A fish when caught needs wine, a live fish needs the river. (Med.)

   A live fish ought to be in the river; a cooked fish should be eaten with wine.

Additional Readings

Audentēs Fortūna juvat.
Fortune aids the daring. (Vergil, *A.* 10.2.84)
   This is another one of the variations of the Basic Sentence, *Fortēs Fortūna adjuvat.*

Ex linguā stultā veniunt incommoda multa.
From a stupid tongue come many inconveniences. (Med.)

Gaudia nōn remanent, sed fugitīva volant.
Joys do not remain, but stealthily fly away. (Martial, 1.15)
   The adjective *fugitīva* seems best translated in English by an adverb.

Corrumpunt bonōs mōrēs colloquia mala.
Evil conversations corrupt good morals. (*I Corinthians* 15.33)
   Talking with people who are evil will corrupt even someone who is intrinsically good.

Dē siccīs lignīs compōnitur optimus ignis.
The best fire is made from dry wood. (Med.)
   You need good material to get good results. "You can't make a silk purse out of a sow's ear."

Praecepta dūcunt, exempla trahunt.
Advice guides people but good examples influence them more strongly. (Med.)

Mors omnia solvit.
Death settles everything. (Legal)

Jūs est in armīs, opprimit lēgēs timor.
Right (now) lies in the force of arms, and fear oppresses the laws. (Seneca, *H.F.* 25)
   This refers to a time of war when the laws had been suspended.

Nātūra nihil facit frūstrā: nōn dēficit in necessāriīs, nec abundat in superfluīs.
Nature does nothing in vain: it is not lacking in necessary things, nor does it abound in superfluous things. (Aristotle, translation, source unknown)
   An early statement about the so-called "balance of nature."

Pendente līte.
While the lawsuit is still not settled. (Legal)

Dant animōs vīna.
Wine gives courage. (Ovid, *Met.* 12.242, adapted)
   The original reads *Vīna dabant animōs.*

Deō favente.
With God's favor. (Commonplace)

UNIT 17

Filmstrip

Everyday Life

Following these notes, a complete English translation of the filmstrip script is given. The teacher is referred to the *Guide to Filmstrip Series RŌMA ANTĪQUA* for additional notes on this filmstrip. The small discrepancy in the filmstrip frame numbers between the reader and the filmstrip guide occurs because the guide includes title and credit frames which are not necessary in the reader.

It is recommended that the filmstrip be shown prior to the students' reading the visually-cued script in *Lēctiōnēs Prīmae*. The filmstrip viewing may be done in several ways. If the teacher chooses to show it to the entire class, the students can then review it in the reader. Another approach is to have individual students or small groups work independently on the filmstrip, either in class or outside, using small table viewers where these are available. The teacher could then show the filmstrip in class and expand with additional comments and explanations, according to his knowledge and ability. Many filmstrip projectors can be manipulated by means of the framing lever so that the caption at the bottom of the frame is not visible. The teacher can then ask questions to probe comprehension of the Latin captions.

This filmstrip can be reinforced by the EBE sound film, "Life in Ancient Rome," to be used either before or after the filmstrip.

1. In the second century A.D. the Roman Empire under the rule of the Emperor Trajan included these countries.
2. Many different peoples live under the Roman rule.
3. An Emperor is being carried in his chariot.
4. Emperors alone held the *imperium*.
5. Trajan is a wise, just, and benevolent Emperor.

61

6. Under the Emperors the Roman Senate held little authority.

7. The Emperor and not the Senate appointed the judges and chief magistrates. Many of these officials came from wealthy families.

8. A few families had the money which was pouring into Rome.

9. These rich citizens own many precious objects.

10. These Roman citizens are eating and drinking with an Arabian trader.

11. The slave girl is giving water; the guest is washing his hands.

12. From all over the world merchants bring precious objects.

13. The Greeks decorate their vases with pictures . . .

14. A luxurious scarlet cloak . . .

15. On the table are gold and silver vessels.

16. Romans, while dining, rested on one elbow.

17. Wealthy people, along with the Emperor, built temples and beautified Rome.

18. The common people did not live in luxurious homes but in dirty tenements called *īnsulae*.

19. These slaves are carrying bags from the portico.

20. The poor are receiving public assistance. The poor want help and not promises of it.

21. The poor person is getting grain from an administrator.

22. Another official gives money.

23. By gifts of grain and by games the Emperors restrain the impoverished populace. Juvenal calls this assistance "bread and circuses."

24. Romans and Greeks possessed many slaves.

25. Fortune makes these women slaves.

26. This slave is teaching his pupils; he is a teacher.

27. This slave wearing trousers is cultivating flowers in the garden.

28. In enormous baths the Romans exercised, bathed, and received massages.

29. These slaves are working in the fields and carrying firewood.

30. Fate makes a man a slave. Cicero says, "Fortune, and not Wisdom, rules our lives."

31. The goddess Diana is concerned for woods and wild animals.

32. For the most part these gods and goddesses come from Greek religion.

33. Jupiter Optimus Maximus is the chief of the gods.

34. At this time only a few good citizens worshipped the ancient gods.

35. Many Romans could not read or write. This professional letter writer is writing a letter for an illiterate man.

36. These citizens at leisure are listening to someone reciting.

37. This author is a senator.

38. He is reciting his works in Latin.

39. In the schools students learned Latin and Greek literature.

40. The Romans preserved the Greek arts: sculpture, architecture, and literature.

41. Through his edicts Trajan ruled this enormous Empire justly.

42. The Roman people saw many spectacles in the Forum.

43. In the Forum are arches, temples, porticoes, columns, and statues.

44. In this modern city (Segovia, Spain) stands this Roman aqueduct. How many enormous arches!

45. The Roman Empire contained many provinces.

46. From the Greeks and Romans the Western world gets its art, literature, and laws. But the Greeks were the inventors and the Romans the preservers.

Questions

1 Quālēs sunt īnsulae ubī habitant inopēs? Sordidae.

2 Quī frūmentum dōnant? Magistrī, administrātōrēs, imperātōrēs.

3 Quālēs hominēs in aedibus sūmptuōsīs habitant? Dīvitēs, opulentī.

4 Quī prō dominīs suīs labōrant? Servī, servae.

5 Quō locō Rōmānī sē lavant? In balneīs.

6 Ā quā deā silvae bēstiaeque cūrantur? Ā Diānā.

7 Quī ā Jove reguntur? Omnēs dī, hominēs.

8 Ā quō opus recitātur? Ab auctōre.

9 Quās rēs continet Forum Rōmānum? Arcūs, templa, porticūs, columnās, statuās.

10 Suntne multae an paucae prōvinciae in Imperiō Rōmānō? Multae.

11 Quālēs litterās docet in scholā magister? Graecās et Latīnās.
12 Estne magister servus an līber? Servus.
(Teachers were usually either slaves or freedmen. The teacher shown in the filmstrip was identified as a slave.)

Readings

1 Knowledge itself is power. (Sir Francis Bacon, *Medit. Sacr. de Haer.?*)

2 Lead becomes gold. (Petronius, 43, adapted)
The Petronius version reads *In manū illīus plumbum aurum fīēbat.* This was the dream of the alchemists, to be able to transmute elements. Although the sentence could also read "Gold becomes lead," it is doubtful that this was the alchemists' goal.

3 No one loves his country because it is big but because it is his own. (Seneca, *Ep.* 66.26)

4 After a disaster, the memory of it is another disaster. (Publilius Syrus)
It is bad enough to undergo some misfortune without tormenting oneself by thinking about it.

5 Kisses, and not eyes, are the leaders in love. (Anon.)
A play on *Oculī in amōre ducēs.* This author says that we do not fall in love by looking at people but after we have kissed them.

6 A pretty face is a silent commendation. (Publilius Syrus)

7 The trip from the earth to the stars is not an easy one. (Seneca, *H.F.* 437)
Because of the kind of life they led, some mortals, such as Hercules, were granted immortality. Both Julius Caesar and Augustus were deified.

8 Hunger is the best cook. (Anon.)

9 No bad man is happy. (Juvenal, 4.8)
Or, "No happy person is bad."

10 Beauty is a fleeting thing. (Seneca, *Ph.* 7.7.3.)

11 God has his hours and his delays. (Anon.)
Sometimes our prayers are answered immediately and sometimes they are not.

12 Virtue is the sole and only kind of nobility. (Juvenal, 8.20)
Or, "Nobility is the sole and only kind of virtue."

13 Old age all by itself is a disease. (Terence, *Ph.* 575)

14 Nothing new under the sun. (*Ecclesiastes* 1.9)

15 Fortune is blind. (Anon.)

16 In human affairs Queen Money is the one who runs the ship. (Med.)

17 A true friend is a rare bird. (Med.)

18 Fortune is never always good. (Burton)

19 Mountaineers are always free. (Motto of West Virginia)

20 Patience is a rare virtue. (Anon.)

21 God is my light. (Motto of Oxford University)

22 Your death is my life. (Anon.)
The idea is that expressed in a Basic Sentence in Unit 22 of the programmed text: "*Mors lupī agnīs vīta*" or "The death of the wolf is life for the lambs."

23 No land is an exile but simply another native land. (Seneca, *De Rem. Fort.* 8.1)

24 Anger without strength to enforce it is empty.
(Anon.)

25 Disaster is never alone. (Anon.)
Troubles never come singly.

26 A good man is a rare creature. (Med.)

27 The present is certain, but the future is uncertain. (Med.)
Notice that *futūra* here is plural.

28 Courage is the only real nobility. (Motto)

29 Education without good morals is useless. (Motto of University of Pennsylvania)

30 The public safety is the supreme law. (Legal)

31 The journey is long through advice, but short and efficient through examples. (Seneca, *Ep.* 6.5)

32 A wise man is the greatest of all miracles. (Hermes Trismegistus?)
Hermes Trismegistus was the supposed author of occult works based on ancient Egyptian lore.

33 The best medicine is moderation. (Anon.)

34 Friendship is just a name, trust is just an empty name. (Ovid, *A.A.* 1.740)
These concepts exist as words but they do not exist in actuality. No one is a true friend.

35 Woman is always a fickle and changeable thing. (Vergil, *A.* 4.569)
In the context of the *Aeneid* this is ironical, since it is Aeneas, the man, who sails away and leaves Dido, the woman.

36 The spirit is willing but the flesh is weak. (*Mark* 14.38)

37 By its nature victory is insolent and haughty. (Cicero, *Pro Marc.* 3.9, adapted)
It is hard to be a good winner.

38 The apple is sweet when the watchman is absent. (Anon.)
   Stolen sweets are best.

39 Necessity is the last and greatest weapon. (Livy, 4.28)

40 He is praised by some, blamed by others. (Horace, *S.*
1.2.11)

41 Love is curable by no herbs. (Ovid, *Met.* 1.523)

42 When a bad man pretends that he is a good man, then he is
at his worst. (Publilius Syrus)

43 After something, because of something. Commonplace
   This is the mistaken belief that, because B follows A,
   A was necessarily the cause of B.

44 When a person is in trouble, scolding him is a cruel thing
to do. (Publilius Syrus)

45 One man, no man. (Med.)
   One man can accomplish nothing by himself.

46 When a joke is true, the joke is a bad thing and a cruel
thing. (Med.)

Additional Readings

Vīna bibunt hominēs, animālia cētera fontēs.
Human beings drink wine, other animals drink water. (Med.)
   Written by someone who was extremely fond of wine.

Multa verba, modica fidēs.
Many words, little belief. (Anon.)
   If a person talks a great deal, we are less inclined to
   believe what he has to say.

Omnia mors aequat.
Death makes everything equal. (Claudian, 35.302)

It is not *omnēs* (which would mean that death makes every*body* equal) but *omnia* (every*thing* equal); people are just the same as animals or vegetables when they die. It was a common Roman view that death was the cessation of everything.

Dēficiente vīnō, dēficit omne.
When wine gives out, then everything gives out. (Rathskeller at Nuremberg)

A Rathskeller is a cellar (German, *Keller*) in a *Rathaus*, which is the town hall, and in this Rathskeller, wine and beer are sold. The term is sometimes used for American restaurants where German food is featured.

Fortūna vitrea est; tum cum splendet frangitur.
Fortune is made of glass; at the time when it shines, it breaks. (Publilius Syrus)

When fortune seems the best, that is the time when it is going to change for the worse.

Labor ipse voluptās.
Hard work is itself a pleasure. (Motto)

This could refer to mental or physical activity.

In hōc sīgnō spēs mea.
My hope is in this sign. (Motto)

Spēs mea Christus.
Christ is my hope. (Motto of Earl of Lucan)

Nūlla sine deō mēns bona est.
There is no noble mind without a god. (Seneca, *Ep.* 73.16)

Nēmō bonus nisī sōlus Deus.
No one is good except God alone. (*Luke* 18.19)

Senectūs enim īnsānābilis morbus est.
Old age is an incurable disease. (Seneca, *Ep.* 108.28)

UNIT 18

Examination

The students might be interested to know that the *Pontus Euxīnus* was originally called *Pontus Axīnus* ("Inhospitable Sea") because of the barbarous tribes surrounding it. Since the Greeks believed that calling something by a bad name possibly made matters worse, they thought it would therefore be helpful to pick a better name. So, just as "The Furies" became "The Well-Disposed Ones," so *Axīnus* became *Euxīnus* ("Hospitable"). Statistics are not available to prove whether this change was beneficial.

About The Roman World

Teacher: What is pictured in this map?

Student: It is Europe.

Teacher: Where is our city Rome?

Student: In Italy.

T: Is Italy an island?

St: No, it is a peninsula.

T: In what way does a peninsula differ from an island?

St: An island is in the middle of a sea or a lake. A peninsula, on the other hand, is almost surrounded by water. Therefore it is not called an *īnsula*, but a *paenīnsula*.

T: What is the name of this large peninsula?

St: Its name is Spain.

T: What is it known for?

St: Many metals are found in this region: gold, silver, bronze, and iron.

T: Are there any famous Spanish people?

St: Yes. The authors Martial and Seneca are from Spain.

T: What is the name of this peninsula?

St: Its Latin name is *Graecia*.

T: How many cities in Greece are particularly famous?

St: Two.

T: What are they?

St: Athens and Sparta.

T: In what region is Athens located?

St: In Attica.

T: And where is Sparta located?

St: In Laconia.

T: What is the largest island?

St: Sicily.

T: What is Sicily known for?

St: On this island the Greeks fought against the Carthaginians and the Carthaginians against the Romans.

T: In what city did the Carthaginians use to live?

St: In the city called Carthage.

T: And what is this large peninsula called?

St: The name is Asia or Asia Minor.

T: Why is it called Asia Minor?

St: The region extending to the Tigris and Euphrates Rivers is also called "Asia."

T: Who lives in Asia Minor?

St: Many nationalities, but particularly Greeks.

T: That's enough about Asia. What is the largest river on this map?

St: The largest is the Nile.

T: Through what region does it flow?

St: Through Egypt.

T: Where does it have its beginning?

St: As Ptolemy the scientist says, there are two different rivers flowing from two lakes. These two rivers make up our Nile.

T: In what way is this Nile River unusual?

St: Every year it rises, floods the land, and then decreases.

T: What does this flooding accomplish?

St: It makes the fields fertile.

T: But if the flood is insufficient, what happens?

St: The grain doesn't grow and there is a famine in Egypt.

T: And if the river does flood?

St: If the water is plentiful, there is prosperity.

T: The Nile helps the Egyptians very much. Do the European rivers give help in a similar way?

St: Two rivers help us, but in a different way.

T: What help do they give?

St: The two rivers defend the state against the barbarians.

T: Which rivers are they?
St: One is the Rhine, the other is the Danube or the Ister.
T: About the Rhine, where does it have its beginning and into what sea does it flow?
St: It flows from the Alps into the German Ocean.
T: But what about the Danube? Why does it have two names?
St: The upper part, flowing from the Alps, is called the Danube and the lower part is called the Ister.
T: What sea receives its waters?
St: The Black Sea.
T: Well done. Your job is over. Good-bye.
St: And good-bye to you, sir.

Questions

The most obvious questions to ask are those which form part of the text, like *"Quid pingitur hāc in tabulā?"* Here, obviously, the students should not refer to their text, since the task would be absurdly simple. On the other hand, to answer without reference to the text is rather difficult. The following questions usually require transformation of the answer given in the text; some also require expansion, and are true "comprehension questions." See pages 9-10 of the Teacher's Manual for *Artēs Latīnae*, Level One.

The use of a wall map will be of great assistance in this Unit and the next.

1 In probātiōne, uter quaerit, magister an discipulus? Magister.
2 Et quid agit discipulus? Respōnsa dat, respondet.
  (*Respondet* has not occurred in either the programmed materials or the reader, but perhaps it has been used in class.)
3 In quā paenīnsulā sunt multa metalla? In Hispāniā.
4 Quae maxima urbs est in Italiā? Rōma.
5 In quā īnsulā pūgnābant Graecī cum Pūnicīs? In Siciliā.
6 Quantum flūmen est Nīlus? Maximum, longum, magnum.
7 Quālēs sunt agrī sī Nīlus crēscit? Fertilēs.
8 Quantum frūmentum in Aegyptō est sī Nīlus dēficit? Parvum, rārum, nōn multum.

71

9 Quae duo flūmina Rōmānōs contrā barbarōs dēfendunt?
Rhēnus et Danūvius vel Ister.
10 Quod in mare fluit Danūvius? In Pontum Euxīnum.

Readings

1 Dropping water wears away a stone, a ring is worn out with use, /and the curved plowshare is ground down by the earth it presses. (Ovid, *Ex P*. 4.10.5-6)
> By constant application, small or weak people may overcome strong obstacles.

2 When a woman weeps she is preparing an ambush with her tears. (Dionysius Cato, 3.20)

3 The gods look on mortal acts with just eyes. (Ovid, *Met*. 13.70)

4 Good friends appear in difficulties. (Anon.)

5 A man by himself is either a god or a beast. (Translation of Aristotle, source unknown)

6 At once said and done. (Anon.)
> "No sooner said than done."

7 Leisure nourishes the body; the mind also is fed by leisure. (Ovid, *Ex P*. 1.4.21)
> Notice that the Latin word *ōtia* is plural.

8 Leisure without reading is death. (Seneca, *Ep*. 82.3)

9 A careless appearance is suitable for men. (Ovid, *A.A.* 1.509)
> In the context Ovid is saying that a man should be neat and clean, but should not spend a lot of money on extravagant dress.

10 Said, done. (Adapted from Terence, *And*. 381)

11 Who holds an eel by the tail does not (really) hold him. (Med.)

12 Nothing is at once discovered and perfected. (Cicero, *Brut.* 70)

13 Past labors are pleasant. (Cicero, *Fin.* 2.32.105)

14 In situations which are particularly unfavorable, harmony is a useful thing. (Anon.)

15 A rolling stone is not covered with moss. (Anon.)

16 A word once spoken flies away and cannot be recovered. (Horace, *Ep.* 1.18.71)
Irreparābile is an adjective modifying *verbum.*

17 Fleeing smoke, he falls into the fire. (Med.)
"Out of the frying pan into the fire."

18 From his foot we can recognize Hercules. (Anon.)

19 One day does not bring spring, nor does one swallow. (Anon.)

20 The end crowns the work. (Med.)
Only when a work is completed can it be said to have merit.

21 God and light. (Motto of Wisconsin)
Through God we see light.

22 Even puppies bite a dead lion. (Med.)
It does not take much courage to kick a man when he is down. A *catulus* is the young of various animals, such as bears, wolves, cats, tigers, and even snakes.

23 Hunger teaches us much. (Anon.)

24 A hungry stomach rarely despises common food. (Horace, *S.* 2.2.38)

25 With God helping. (Motto)

26 Truth conquers all. (Motto)

27 A great city is a great solitude. (Anon.)
One can be lonelier in a large city than anywhere else.

28 Love is the best teacher. (Pliny, *Ep.* 4.19.5, adapted)

29 In flight, death is disgraceful; in victory, it is glorious.
(Cicero, *Phil.* 14.12.32)

30 Wine is one thing, drunkenness is something else. (Anon.)

31 No one is content with his lot. (Anon.)

32 Rule over good people is easy. (Plautus, *Mil. Glor.* 611)

33 Who is the poor man? The miser. (Pseudo-Ausonius)

34 Every beginning is difficult. (Anon.)

35 In all things the first undertaking is hard. (Anon.)

36 They turn black into white. (Juvenal, 3.30)
They can convince you that black is white.

37 The times need a leader. (Lucan, 7.88, adapted)
The actual quotation of Lucan is a negative one, *Sī mīlite Magnō nōn duce tempus eget,* which means, "If the times do not need the soldier Pompey the Great as a leader." Notice again how often the Latin uses a different number than the English.

38 No day lacks sorrow. (Med.)

39 A woman who comes with a dowry controls her husband. (Anon.)
The students must know that a dowry is the money, goods, or estate which a woman brings to her husband at marriage. With this as a lever she could exercise power over

him which a woman without a dowry could not. Customs about dowries vary in different countries; in some places, if a woman leaves her husband, she is entitled to have her dowry returned to her.

40 For many are called, but few are chosen. (*Matthew* 20, 16)

41 He is praised not without reason but without end. (Anon.)
We do not mind his receiving praise; it is just the fact that he gets too much.

42 When the older generation makes mistakes, the younger generation learns bad habits. (Publilius Syrus)

43 Every prosperity is unstable and uncertain. (Seneca, *Controv.* 1.1.3)

44 Courage is a thousand shields. (Motto)
A man who is courageous is worth a thousand soldiers equipped with shields.

45 My mind is like a clean tablet. (Renaissance; Pauli?)

46 Many lose their own belongings while they greedily seek the belongings of others. (Anon.)

47 The highest law is often the highest evil. (Terence, *Heaut.* 796)
The highest laws are the most general and therefore the most inflexible.

Poems

Baths, wine, and Venus destroy our bodies.
But baths, wine, and Venus are what make life worthwhile.
(Buechler, 1499)

This inscription will indicate how dear to the Roman heart was the ritual of the baths, with their attendant exercise grounds, library, etc. Our corresponding phrase is, "Wine women, and song."

This is my eternal home
and everlasting happiness;
and of all my possessions
this alone is really mine.
(*Corpus Inscriptionum Latinarum* 8.10927)

Namely, my tomb.

As Proserpina, goddess of the dead, she terrifies the people in
the underworld with her scepter. As Luna, the moon goddess,
she illuminates the upper world with her brightness. And as
Diana, the goddess of the hunt, she drives wild animals with
her arrow. (Anon.)

These lines illustrate beautifully the difficulties of translation. Diana is spoken of in her three guises: as Proserpina,
goddess of the underworld; as Luna, the moon goddess;
and as the goddess of the hunt.

The number of complete poems increases as more structures
become available. It is recommended that the teacher cover at
least one of these poems in class in each Unit. There will be
others, however, which will be too difficult for the slower
students in many high school classes.

Additional Readings

Homō sōlus aut deus aut daemōn.
A man who lives by himself is either a god or a devil. (Anon.)
Living in solitude will work such change in a person's
character that either he will become a saint or just the
opposite.

Crēdula est spēs improba.
Credulous hope is wicked. (Seneca, *Th.* 295)
The Romans were fond of saying that hope is a bad thing
because it never comes up to our expectations; we are
always disappointed.

Nihil est ab omnī parte beātum.
Nothing is desirable from every point of view. (Horace, *O.*
2.16.28)

76

Nīl perpetuum, pauca diūturna sunt.
Nothing lasts forever, few things last for a long time. (Seneca, *De Consol.* 1.1)

Philosophia . . . et contemplātīva est et āctīva: spectat simul agitque.
Philosophy is both contemplative and active: at the same time it both observes and it acts. (Seneca, *Ep.* 95.10)
This refers to an argument of ancient times. One group held that the true task of a philosopher was merely to think; the other held that he should take an active part in public affairs and put his philosophy to practical use in his daily living.

Omnis amor caecus; nōn est amor arbiter aequus.
All love is blind; love is not a fair judge. (Med.)

"Sufficit" et "Satis est." Sīc numquam dīcit avārus.
"It is sufficient" and "That is enough." This is what the miser never says. (Med.)

Nihil in studiīs parvum est.
In studies nothing is of small account. (Anon.)

Vir duplex animō incōnstāns est in omnibus viīs suīs.
A double-minded man is unstable in all his ways. (*James* 1.8)

Mulier malum necessārium.
Woman is a necessary evil. (Anon.)

Omnis habet sua dōna diēs.
Every day has its own gifts. (Anon.)

In marī magnō piscēs capiuntur.
Fish are caught in a large sea. (Anon.)

Amphora sub veste rārō portātur honestē.
A jar is rarely carried under a person's coat for an honorable reason. (Med.)

UNIT 19

Examination

About Italy[1]

Teacher: What is pictured in this map?
Student: This map describes Italy.
T: What sort of a country is Italy?
St: In this peninsula, teacher, there are large mountain
ranges.
T: How many mountain ranges are there?
St: Two.
T: What are these two ranges?
St: The largest are the Alps.
T: Where are the Alps?
St: In upper Italy.
T: How do these mountains help us?
St: They defend Italy well against its enemies.
T: How many lakes are there in the Alps?
St: Three large, beautiful ones.
T: What are their names?
St: Lake Maggiore, Lake Como, Lake Garda.
T: Who lives there?
St: Many rich Romans have villas on the shores.
T: What is the other mountain range?
St: The Apennines, which take up almost all of Italy.
T: Are there no plains?
St: Between the Alps and the Apennines is a plain which is
large and fertile.
T: What is the river in this plain?
St: The Po, which flows from the Alps into the Adriatic Sea.
T: How many other large rivers are there?

---

[1] Teachers familiar with Latin poetry may wonder at the initial short /i/ of *Italia*. The short /i/ is correct in prose. The form *Ītalia* is used in poetry as a result of Greek influence.

St: Sir, Italy has few large rivers. There is however a well-known river named the Tiber which flows through Rome itself.
T: Into what sea does the Tiber flow?
St: Into the *Mare Tyrrhēnum* or the *Mare Tuscum*.
T: This sea has two names. Why?
St: *Tyrrhēnus* and *Tuscus* are other words for "Etruscan."
T: Where did the Etruscans live?
St: In the Sixth Century B.C. they possessed the largest part of Italy.
T: At that time who ruled the other sections of Italy?
St: Various people, who were called *Italī*, held the middle part.
T: And who lived in the lower part?
St: Many Greeks. From this fact the region was called *Magna Graecia*.
T: That's enough, student.[1] Good-bye.
St: Thank you, sir; good-bye to *you*.

Questions

The examination on geography continues. The questions below are in addition to the questions within the text. The beginning teacher should notice in what way some questions are more difficult than others. (See Unit 18 for references to the Teacher's Manual.) Even with no experience in forming questions, the beginning teacher should by now be able to make up some of his own. As before, he should use a map.

1 Quam paenīnsulam videt discipulus in tabulā? Italiam.
2 Quibus in montibus sunt lacūs Verbannus, Lārius, Bēnācus? In Alpibus.
3 Quī mōns mediam Italiam occupat? Mōns Appennīnus.
4 Per quam urbem fluit Tiberis? Per Rōmam.
5 Quod mare accipit Tiberim flūmen? Mare Tyrrhēnum vel Tuscum.
6 Quae duae vōcēs quoque sīgnificant "Etruscus"? "Tyrrhēnus" et "Tuscus."
7 Quō tempore rēgnābant Etruscī? Saeculō sextō ante Christum nātum.

---

[1] An American teacher would be more likely to use the student's name.

79

8 Ā quibus tenēbātur Italia īnferior? Ā Graecīs.
9 Quō locō est Magna Graecia? In Italiā īnferiōre.

Readings

1 It is not a good idea for a person who has flour in his mouth
to blow a flame out. (Med.)
> There are times when certain actions are inappropriate and
> offensive. The use of *bene* with a verb in a proverb is often
> best translated as above.

2 Who becomes wise through someone else's difficulties becomes wise in a happy fashion. (Plautus, *Merc.* 4.7.40)
> He doesn't have to pay the price of learning through his
> *own* trial and error what to do and what not to do.

3 Who conquers anger conquers his greatest enemy. (Publilius
Syrus)

4 Not all people who have a lyre are lyre players. (Varro,
R.R. 2.1.3)

5 Who suffers a shipwreck a second time unjustly accuses
Neptune. (Publilius Syrus)
> If you have suffered a misfortune, and try the same thing
> again, you have only yourself to blame if misfortune oc-
> curs once more.

6 What the helmsman is in a ship, what the driver is in a
chariot, what the leader is in a chorus, and finally what law
is in a state and a leader in the army, that is what God is in the
world. (Translation of Aristotle)
> Notice the variant form *nāvī* in place of *nāve*. Once the
> student has seen this variant form, the teacher should
> accept either the form *nāve* or *nāvī*.

7 The judge who punishes an innocent man condemns himself. (Publilius Syrus)

8 The sick man who makes his doctor his heir does himself a disservice. (Publilius Syrus)

His doctor is apt to poison him.

9 Who makes an old man his heir puts his treasure in the grave. (Publilius Syrus)

There is no point in leaving money to an old man, because he will soon die.

10 Even a thorn bush is pleasant, from which a rose is seen. (Publilius Syrus)

Difficult situations are not unpleasant if they lead to something desirable. Disagreeable parents may have attractive children.

11 Where the person who accuses is (also) the person who judges, violence, not law, prevails. (Publilius Syrus)

12 The timid person sees even dangers which do not exist. (Publilius Syrus)

13 There are as many sorrows in love as there are rabbits in the field. (Med.)

14 They condemn what they do not understand. (Anon.)

15 Who runs away from the millstone, runs away from the flour. (Anon.)

If you do not want to work, you do not get the rewards of work.

16 The stupid person conceals nothing: he reveals what he has in his heart. (Med.)

17 Many promise in the evening what they refuse the next morning. (Med.)

18 Opportunity is presented rarely, and is easily lost. (Publilius Syrus)

19 The person who is a miser is always in want. (St. Jerome, *Ep.* 100.15)

20 The person who sees his own acts does not make fun of me. (Anon.)

21 There are as many opinions as there are people. (Anon.)
Caput is often used in Latin for counting people. In English, we also speak of a "head count" with reference to people, and of so many "head" of cattle, in speaking about animals.

22 An example accomplishes nothing that solves one controversy by introducing another. (Horace, *S.* 2.3.103)
There are some explanations which only introduce new difficulties and therefore are useless.

23 How happy is a life which is spent without hatred! (Publilius Syrus)

24 A person does not smell good who always smells good. (Martial 2.12)
Martial does not approve of excessive use of perfume.

25 Greed increases as much as your money increases. (Med.)

26 What is true, is safe. (Anon.)

27 Who takes a wife, takes trouble and strife. (Med.)

28 Who desires nothing has everything. (Valerius Maximus, 4.4.1)
Applied to the famous Cornelia who displayed her children and said, "These are my jewels."

29 It goes badly with a master whom the foreman instructs. (Anon.)
The *vīlicus* was the person in charge of a farm; if he must tell the farm owner how to run his business, the farm is not going to prosper.

30 Whatever is done with courage is done with glory. (Publilius Syrus)

31 Everything which is covered by snow appears when the snow disappears. (Med.)
   You can hide the truth just so long but eventually it comes to light. Compare our expression about sweeping things under the rug.

32 Neither rashly nor timidly. (Family motto)
   Note the short /e/ at the end of *temere*. Lewis and Short's dictionary is in error here in marking it long. Because of the collateral form *temeriter*, we would class *temere* as an adverb with the /e/ short, as in *bene* and *male*.

33 The person who runs away from hard work is not a brave and active man. (Seneca, *Ep.* 22.7)

34 As the master is, so is the servant. (Petronius, 58)

35 Happy is the person whom other people's dangers make cautious. (Med.)

36 Whom he likes, he likes; whom he does not like, he does not like. (Petronius, 37)
   A man who knows his own mind.

37 Not everyone who is called wise is wise, but rather he who learns and retains wisdom. (Petrus Alphonsus)

38 Who captures is himself captured. (Anon.)
   If you hunt a lion, you may get eaten yourself.

39 There is no bad person who is not foolish. (Burton)
   This is the idea that virtue is synonymous with wisdom.

40 What the gods want comes to pass quickly. (Petronius, 76)

41 Whoever desires is always poor. (Claudian, *In Rufin.* 1.200)
   This is the Stoic doctrine that true wealth consists of freedom from desire for material possessions.

42 Virtue gives what beauty denies. (Motto)
If you are not good-looking, you can win admiration by your actions.

43 No one attacks me with impunity. (Motto of Black Watch)
Anyone who harms me will be punished.

44 Who sows sparingly also reaps sparingly. (*II Corinthians* 9.6)
Greek has the corresponding word for *metit* in the future; in Latin either present or future is correct.

45 Who weighs his own faults does not condemn mine. (Med.)

46 The mouth, the eyes, the expression betray what the heart has inside. (Med.)

47 What is not learned in one's youth is not known at a mature age. (Cassiodorus, *Var.* 1.24)

48 What is good is suppressed, but never extinguished. (Publilius Syrus)

Poems

While Poggio praises his homeland and condemns the enemy, he is a good citizen and a bad historian. (Sannazaro)

In English, to say that someone is "not bad" is faint praise; in Latin, this figure of speech (called "litotes") that says one thing by denying its opposite is used as a stronger mode of expression. *Nec bonus historicus* therefore means that he was a bad, very bad, historian.

There are as many teachers as there are flowers in the springtime;/there are as many errors as nature has colors. (Med.)

This sort of medieval verse with internal rhyme, like *doctōrēs ... flōrēs*, is called "Leonine verse."

"There are thirty bad epigrams in the whole book."/If there are that many good ones, Lausus, it is a good book. (Martial 7.81)

The epigrams of Martial appear in books, each consisting of about 100 epigrams. Martial says elsewhere that one third of his epigrams are good, one third are bad, and one third are mediocre, and that this is about as high a percentage as you can expect from anyone.

Smyrna, Chios, Colophon, Salamis, Rhodes, Argos, Athens,/and the whole world argue about your native land (claim you as their own). (Translation of the *Greek Anthology* 6.298)

In connection with the dialogue on geography, even the slower students might be interested in this poem.

There are *eight* places which claim Homer: the seven cities plus the whole world. Thomas Seward (1708-1790) put it this way:
Seven wealthy towns contend for Homer dead,
Through which the living Homer begged his bread.

The "Homeric Question" is more complicated than explained to the student and may be summarized by saying that there is not yet agreement on how much any. one man (whom we may call "Homer") is responsible for the *Iliad* and the *Odyssey*.

Additional Readings

Neque mel neque apēs.
Neither honey nor bees. (Anon.)
If you do not work, you will not get any reward. Also, when there is no danger (bees), there is no pleasure (honey).

Verba volant, scrīpta manent.
Spoken words fly away, written words remain. (Anon.)

Suō . . . ūnus quisque studiō maximē dūcitur.
Each person is particularly led by his own desire. (Cicero, *Fin.* 5.2.5)

Quī facit per alterum facit per sē.
Who does something through someone else does it through himself. (Legal)

A man is responsible for what he gets somebody else to do for him. This agent, in legal parlance, is called a "particeps criminis."

Nōn capit rēgnum duōs.
A kingdom cannot contain two rulers. (Seneca, *Th.* 444)

Quae est maxima egestās? Avāritia.
What is the greatest poverty? Greed. (Pseudo-Seneca)
> The miser can never get enough, no matter how much he already has.

Vīna parant animōs.
Wine prepares the emotions. (Ovid. *A.A.* 1.237)

Amīcitia inter pōcula contracta plērumque est vitrea.
A friendship which is made in the midst of drinking glasses usually is made of glass. (Med.)
> Like the glasses, it will easily break.

Malevolus animus abditōs dentēs habet.
A malevolent spirit has hidden teeth. (Publilius Syrus)

Homō doctus in sē semper dīvitiās habet.
A learned man always has riches within himself. (Phaedrus, 4.19)
> Wisdom is his wealth.

Haec ratiō perfecta virtūs vocātur.
This perfect reason is called virtue. (Seneca, *Ep.* 76.10)

Āmissīs rēbus, nēmō sapiēns.
When money is lost, nobody is wise. (Med.)
> No one is considered wise if he has lost his money.

UNIT 20

Story

It is essential to recognize that in teaching mythology we must not expurgate the stories to the point where they become meaningless. It is less than honest to tell the story of Hercules and the snakes without some explanation of the hostility of Juno. Many textbooks have failed to explain the background of myths sufficiently, and thus the story seems incredible. Students would ask, naturally, "Why did Juno want to kill a poor little baby?"

Mature students will enjoy reading Plautus' comedy *Amphitryon*, which clearly indicates the lack of belief in the old mythology.

The ancient authors were not bothered by inconsistencies. Odysseus is a hero in Homer, a villain in Vergil. Sophocles takes both sides: in the *Philoctetes* Odysseus is a villain, in the *Ajax* a hero. The "standard received" version of mythology in our texts is often based on Ovid.

Juno Sends Dangers to Hercules

Two baby brothers are asleep. But Hercules is lying in a shield. A shield is a fit place for mighty Hercules!

Look! Two snakes are coming, sent by Juno. They crawl to the shield, where Hercules is lying. What a danger for the sleeping child! Awakened from his sleep, he seizes the two snakes, squeezes them hard and kills them in this way. His brother Iphicles however in terror shouts loudly and arouses his parents. The father, carrying a light, and the mother are afraid for Hercules and Iphicles and seek their children. "Why does our Iphicles shout?" cries Alcmena.

Suddenly they see Hercules with the dead snakes. "Our children are now safe." But angry Juno will send[1] many other dangers to Hercules.

Questions

1 Uter īnfāns in scūtō dormit, Iphiclēs an Herculēs? Herculēs.
2 Quem īnfantem tenet scūtum? Herculem.
3 Quis anguēs mittit? Jūnō.
4 Quem petunt hae vīperae? Herculem, īnfantem fortem.
5 Uter īnfāns timōre excitātus clāmat? Iphiclēs.
6 Uter īnfāns fortiter agit? Herculēs.
7 Quibus membrīs Herculēs anguēs necat? Manibus.
8 Quibus timent pater māterque? Īnfantibus, Herculī et Iphiclī.
9 Ā quō fertur lūmen? Ā patre.
10 Quī salvī sunt? Īnfantēs, frātrēs, Herculēs Iphiclēsque.
11 Quī mortuī sunt? Vīperae, anguēs.

Readings

1 One's own seems handsome to each person. (Cicero, *Tusc.* 5.22.63)

2 Even rabbits insult a dead lion. (Anon.)
   Or, "Even rabbits dance on a dead lion."

3 Nothing is difficult for the brave and faithful. (Motto)

4 Faithful to king and country. (Motto)

5 The person whom Fortune favors has many friends. (Anon.)

6 For another human being, a human being is either a god or a wolf. (Erasmus)
   This quotation resembles closely the reading on the test for Unit 21.

---

[1] The future tense *mittet* is explained.

7 Many things are lacking to poverty; everything is lacking to greed. (Publilius Syrus)

8 For a stupid man silence is a substitute for wisdom. (Publilius Syrus)

9 An ant is pleasing to an ant, and a grasshopper to another grasshopper. (Translation of Theocritus)

10 A king is a person who fears nothing,
   a king is a person who desires nothing;
   this kingdom each person gives himself.
   (Seneca, *Thyest.* 388)
      This is the Stoic doctrine that the wise man is king.

11 Nothing is sure for mankind. (Ovid, *Tr.* 5.5.27)

12 For God does not do everything for mankind. (Seneca, *N.Q.* 7.30.3)

13 No faith is put in a person who does not have money. (Ausonius, *Epigr.* 92.4)

14 Nothing is difficult for the lover. (Cicero, *Or.* 10.33)

15 Nothing flourishes forever: one generation succeeds another generation. (Cicero, *Phil.* 11.15.39)

16 One's own day of death is set for each person. (Vergil, *A.* 10.467)

17 Faithful to God and King. (Motto)

18 Anger which one friend generates for another friend dies down quickly. (Med.)

19 Even a sheep, if it is injured, fights back against someone who threatens it. (Propertius, 2.5.20)

20 And now truth is commonly attributed to wine. (Pliny, *N.H.* 14.141)

21 The highest position does not hold two people. (Anon.)

22 What is the blind man doing with the mirror? (Med.)
   Caecō is dative case.

23 Every country is a native land for one who is brave. (Ovid, *F.* 1.493)

24 Who is mine is dear to me, who is someone else's is dear to him. (Plautus, *Capt.* 400)

25 A miser lacks as much what he has as what he does not have. (Publilius Syrus)
   Avārō is dative case; *quod habet* is the subject of *dēest*.

26 For one who is happy, every country is a native land. (Anon.)

27 How similar to friendship is flattery! (Seneca, *Ep.* 45)

28 No day is long for the person who is active. (Seneca, *Ep.* 122.3)

29 To one who does nothing the day is long. (Seneca? Misquote of *Ep.* 122.3?)

30 Glory comes late to the ashes. (Martial, 1.25.8)
   "Ashes" here refers to the corpse which has been burned. If you become famous only when you're dead, it's too late to do you any good.

31 Poor in the midst of great riches. (Horace, *O.* 3.16.28)
   The person is poor, even though rich, because he is greedy for more.

32 There is eternal prosperity for no man. (Plautus, *Curc.* 189)

33 A word to the wise is enough. (Plautus, *Pers.* 4.11.17)

34 There are as many opinions as there are men; each one has his own way of doing things. (Terence, *Phorm.* 454)

More literally, the last clause is "one's own custom to each one."

35 He gives late who gives to one who asks. (Anon.)
We should give before we are asked.

36 Belief is not given to a liar even when he tells the truth. (Adapted from Cicero, *Div.* 2.146)

37 To whom money is lacking, to him all things are lacking. (Anon.)

38 The robber passes by the poor man; even in a road that is besieged there is peace for the poor man.
(Seneca?)

39 Patience is a remedy for any grief you wish. (Publilius Syrus)

40 For a free-born man, debt is a form of slavery. (Publilius Syrus)
Aliēnum aes ("somebody else's money") is the Latin expression for debt.

41 What unhappy people want too much, this they easily believe. (Seneca, *H.F.* 318-19)

42 Both the highwayman and the cautious traveller are equipped with a sword/but the former is carrying it as an ambush and the latter is carrying it to assist himself. (Ovid, *R.* 2.271)

43 A person's own way of life creates his fortune for him. (Cornelius Nepos, *Att.* 11.19)
Nepos is quoting an unknown poet.

44 Conscience places reins upon our tongue.
(Publilius Syrus)

45 As far as I am concerned, the person is not wise who is wise in his speech but the person who is wise in his deeds. (Gregory, quoted by Burton)

46 Every envious person is absent, if you do not have prosperity. (Anon.)

47 The person who does not put reins upon his mouth often suffers a penalty. (Med.)

48 The person who accommodates himself to necessity is wise. (Anon.)

Poems

While my purse jingles, then the host brings me courses of food;/when my purse is empty, the host does not bring me any courses of food. (Med.)

Rumor creates more rumors, mistake creates more mistakes, just as a small ball of snow increases by rolling. (Owen)

The writer is John Owen, whose epigrams were published in 1624.

Additional Readings

Quī nōn dat quod amat nōn accipit ille quod optat.
Who does not give what he likes does not receive what he wants. (Med.)

Facile perit amīcitia coācta.
A forced friendship is easily destroyed. (Anon.)

Nōn semper homō tālis est quālis dīcitur.
A person is not always the kind of person he is said to be. (Med.)

Nēmō hunc amat quī verba nūntiat mala.
No one likes the person who brings bad news. (Med.)

Nēmo diū gaudet quī jūdice vincit inīquō.
No one is happy very long who wins (his lawsuit) through an unjust judge. (Dionysius Cato, 2.14)

Quis dīves? Quī nīl cupit. Quis pauper? Avārus.
Who is rich? The person who desires nothing. Who is poor?
The greedy man. (Seneca?)

Quod nātūra negat, nēmō fēlīciter audet.
No one successfully dares to do that which nature denies him.
(Anon.)
> If you are not competent to do something, you are asking
> for trouble if you attempt it.

Nōbilis est ille quem nōbilitat sua virtūs.
The person is noble whom his own virtue makes noble. (Med.)

Est bene vestūtus quī sē virtūtibus ōrnat.
The person who adorns himself with virtues is well-dressed.
(Med.)

Numquam nimis dīcitur quod numquam satis discitur.
A thing which is not learned sufficiently is never said too much.
(Anon.)

Quī sua dat lārgē, laudātur ab omnibus ille.
Who gives his possessions generously is praised by all. (Med.)

Nēmō est amātor quisquis nōn semper amat.
No one is a lover who does not always love. (Translation of
Aristotle)
> Love is not something you can put on and take off; it must
> be continuous.

UNIT 21

Story

Again, an explanation of the background is essential to understand the story. Students used to ask, "If Hercules was so strong, why didn't he throw Eurystheus out instead of bothering with these labors?" The introduction in the student's reader explains why.

The students should locate Argos and Mycenae on a map.

About the Labors of Hercules[1]

Against his will Hercules serves Eurystheus. The king gives Hercules twelve labors. "Here is your first labor. In the Nemean Wood near Mycenae is a lion who is harming men and beasts. All the fields have been laid waste. The farmers fear for their lives. Kill this Nemean lion for me."

Hercules journeys to this forest which is called Nemea. He quickly finds the lion, draws his bow, and lets go his arrows. But because the lion's skin is extremely strong, they do not harm the Nemean lion. The hero takes up his club, which he always carries with him and beats the beast. The lion flees to his cave.

Hercules also enters the cave and after a brief struggle in its entrance, strangles the lion. He places the dead beast upon his shoulders and returns to Eurystheus. "The first labor has been accomplished by me," he says. "The Nemean lion is dead. What is the second labor?"

This success does not please Eurystheus, who is terrified by such bravery. "Kill the Hydra of Lerna for me!" "No sooner said than done," replies Hercules.

---

[1]*Herculeī* is an adjective modifying *labōribus.*

Lerna is a lake near Mycenae in which lives a remarkable monster which has seven heads. The hero, now always clad in the lion's skin, hurries to this lake with his friend Iolaus. Without delay he attacks the Hydra with arrows, but the skin is like the lion's skin. Therefore with a mighty blow he knocks off one head of the seven with his club. But in vain! Now *two* heads grow in place of a single head.

Iolaus however gives help to Hercules. He builds a fire, heats some iron, and with this burning iron sears the wounds. Because of this action the heads no longer grow, the monster is killed, and our hero Hercules again is victor.

In the third labor Hercules hunts a deer which has golden horns and runs with unbelievable swiftness. For a whole year the man chases the deer. Finally, by means of a pitfall, he captures the beast, which he brings back alive to the king.

The fourth, sixth, and seventh labors are like the third. In these he captures animals which are harmful to men. In the fourth he captures a ferocious boar; in the sixth, birds which are killing men; in the seventh, mares which eat human flesh.

In the fifth labor, however, Hercules cleanses the stables which King Augeas possesses. He accomplishes this difficult task by using his mind and not his hands. For he diverts the Alpheus River from its course through the stables, which in this manner become cleansed.

Although all these verb forms have been translated by an English present, there is no reason a past tense could not have been used. Thus it is quite correct to say, "Against his will Hercules *served* Eurystheus, etc." A Latin writer, on the other hand, would not have used the historical present for such an extended period of time as has been done here. Perhaps the use of the English present underlines the artificiality of the language used in these stories, since they use only part of the structures which are found in Latin. It is equally odd to read so long a Latin passage which contains no subjunctive. This restricted use of structures is one of the inherent difficulties of "made Latin."

Questions

1 Quōs laedit leō Nemeaeus? Hominēs et bēstiās.
2 Quō īnstrūmentō pulsat Herculēs leōnem? Fūste.
3 Quālis pellis Herculem vestit? Leōnīna, dūra.
4 Quālem pellem possidet Hydra? Similem pellī leōnīnae; dūram.
5 Quis Herculem contrā Hydram adjuvat? Īolāus, amīcus.
6 Quem in locum cadit cervus? In foveam.
7 Quae animālia carnem hūmānam edunt? Equae.
8 Quō auxiliō Herculēs stabula sordida pūrgat? Mente; flūmine Alpheō.
9 Hāc in fābulā quot labōrēs cōnficit Herculēs? Septem.
   (Although the students have not had all the numerals, the word *septem* occurred in the reading.)

Readings

1 Death threatens all. (Common grave inscription)

2 Solitude pleases the Muses, the city is unfriendly for poets. (Petrarch?)

3 The sun shines upon us all. (Petronius, 100)

4 God does not give everything to everybody. (Med.)

5 Her own king pleases a queen. (Plautus, *Stich.* 133)

6 Flame is next to the fire. (Plautus, *Curc.* 53)
   Where there's smoke, there's fire; where there's rumor, there's apt to be some kind of truth.

7 A common shipwreck is a consolation for everybody. (Anon.)
   A disaster is easier to bear when it is shared with others.

8 To the pure all things are pure. (*Titus* 1.15)

9 The river which has been stirred up furnishes opportunity to fishermen. (Med.)

10 Different things please different people. (Anon.)

11 He who is not an unpleasant teacher is dear to children. (Med.)

12 Fortune is given to brave men. (Ennius, *A.* 247)

13 Nothing is difficult for lovers. (St. Jerome, *Ep.* 22.40)

14 That which is pleasing to many people is guarded with the greatest danger. (Publilius Syrus)

15 Violence is hostile to the laws. (Legal)

16 Vices are close to virtues. (St. Jerome, *Adv. Lucif.* 15)
The difference between vices and virtues is sometimes hard to see. Caution is a virtue, cowardice is a vice, and yet what one person might call caution, another might call cowardice.

17 God resists the proud, but grants grace to the humble. (*I Peter* 5.6)

18 For those who are extraordinary, youth is short and old age uncommon. (Martial 6.29.7)

19 Not for ourselves alone. (Motto)

20 Justice for all. (Motto of District of Columbia)

21 Fortune favors the stupid. (Anon.)

22 For God, for country, for friends. (Motto)

23 Different things seem best to different people. (Attributed to Cicero)

24 That land pleases me in which a small piece of property makes me happy (or prosperous).
To the practical Romans, the word *beātus* meant both "happy" and "rich."

25 What is food for some people is bitter poison for others. (Anon.)

26 Who forgives one fault, persuades more people to make similar errors. (Publilius Syrus)

27 Benefits are not welcome which are accompanied by fear. (Publilius Syrus)
>   More literally, "Benefits are unwelcome for whom fear is a companion."

28 For all things, virtue, fame, honor, things divine and human, are obedient to beautiful riches. (Horace, *S.* 2.3.94-96)
>   Horace is speaking cynically here.

29 Whoever during his lifetime takes care of his parents, this person both living and dead is dear to the gods. (Translation of Stobaeus)

30 Not even Jupiter is pleasing to everyone. (Translation of Theognis)

31 What is pleasant for some is bitter for others. (Anon.)

32 The seas are tried after a shipwreck. (Anon.)
>   He is making another voyage after a shipwreck. It is foolish to run a risk a second time.

33 Whoever flees from his family flees a long way. (Petronius, 43)
>   The ties of family are so strong that it is almost impossible to go far enough away to escape them.

34 Money which has been piled up either commands or obeys each person. (Horace, *Ep.* 1.10.47)
>   Money is a good servant but a bad master.

35 As a man is, so is his speech. (Anon.)
>   You can judge a man from what he says.

36 In this kind of river these kinds of fish are caught. (Med.)

37 Who wants all, loses all. (Anon.)

38 As the father is, so is the son. (Anon.)

39 As many fish as there are in the sea, as many birds as are covered by foliage,/as many stars as the sky holds, so many girls does your Rome hold. (Ovid. *A.A.* 1.58-59)

40 Who praises his own family, praises what belongs to others. (Seneca, *H.F.* 344-5)
> The glory belongs to his ancestors, not to him.

41 There are as many enemies as there are slaves. (Festus?)
> Slaves inevitably hate their masters.

42 Wise is he who looks ahead. (Motto of Malvern College)

Poems

Because the crowd dressed in their togas shouts such a loud "Well done" for you,/it is not you, Pomponius, who is learned but your dinner. (Martial, 6.48)

> They applaud him when he recites poetry with his dinner, in order to get invited again to dinner, not because they like the poetry.

In his will Faustinus, Crispus did not leave a cent to his wife. "Whom did he give it to then?" To himself. (Martial, 5.32)

> He spent all his money on himself before he died.

Additional Readings

Peccātum duplicat quī sē dē crīmine jactat.
The person who boasts about his crime doubles his mistake. (Med.)

Stultī quī crēscunt stultī sunt quandō senēscunt.
Those who grow up foolish are foolish when they become old. (Med.)

99

Just because a person is older does not necessarily mean that he is wise.

Fāma bona lentē volat et mala fāma repente.
Good news flies slowly and bad news flies swiftly. (Med.)

Prīnceps quī dēlātōrēs nōn castīgat irrītat.
The ruler who does not punish his informers encourages them. (Suetonius, *Dom.* 9.3)

A *dēlātōr* was an informer who was rewarded for bringing information to the attention of the authorities. Informers should be punished, not rewarded, because rewards only inflame (*irrītat*) their desire for more rewards. Curiously enough, this was the saying of the Emperor Domitian who was notorious for the use he made of informers.

Homō hominī deus est.
For a human being, a man is a god. (Caecilius, quoted by Symmachus, *Ep.* 9.114.1)

Levis est labor omnis amantī.
Every labor is easy for one who is in love. (Med.)

Māter dat puerō propriō quod nōn aliēnō.
A mother gives to her own son what she does not give to someone else's son. (Med.)

Probō bona fāma maxima est hērēditās.
For an honest person the best inheritance is a good reputation. (Publilius Syrus)

Rēx est mendīcus cui nōn est ūllus amīcus.
A king for whom there is no other friend is a beggar. (Med.)
A king without a friend is no better than a beggar.

Nec rejicit quemquam philosophia nec ēligit; omnibus lūcet.
Philosophy neither rejects anyone nor chooses anyone; it shines on all. (Seneca, *Ep.* 44.2)

Mortuīs mala nūlla sunt.
There are no evils for the dead. (Seneca, *Cons. Marc.* 19)

Et mala sunt vīcīna bonīs.
Even bad things are close to good ones. (Med.)
This is the same thought as that expressed in an earlier reading in this Unit.

UNIT 22

Story

About Other Labors of Hercules[1]

Such successes of the hero Hercules did not please Eurystheus. In terror he hid himself in an immense vase and did not receive Hercules within the walls of the city. To Hercules standing outside of the walls of the city he shouted, "Bring me the belt of Hippolyte!"

For Hippolyte ruled the Amazons, who were female warriors. Hercules conquered her, although she fought bravely, and brought the belt back to the king.

In the tenth labor he fought in Spain against the monster Geryon, and after a fierce battle was victorious. Then he brought the bulls of Geryon through Europe to Greece, a journey of the greatest difficulty.

Eurystheus put an eleventh labor on Hercules: "Seek for me the apples which the Hesperides grow." These Hesperides were the three daughters of Hesperus, who lived in Africa. These apples were golden. A dragon who never slept guarded them. Hercules killed the dragon, took the three golden apples, and gave them to King Eurystheus.

Now Eurystheus was almost without hope. "Hercules has completed all the labors placed upon him. What is the labor of the greatest danger?" Suddenly he got an idea. From the walls of his city he ordered Hercules: "Oh, brave and faithful one, go down to the Underworld. This journey for you doubtless will be easy. Bring back to me alive the dog Cerberus. After this deed your labors will be completed. After the journey to

---

[1]Here all historical present tenses are translated by English past tenses.

101

the Underworld, Hercules, good, noble, and brave, will rest."
He laughed cruelly, for the death of Hercules now seemed
certain. His plan pleased Eurystheus exceedingly.

Even Hercules, when he heard the words of the king, grew pale.
Who wouldn't fear such dangers? But he replied: "For Hercu-
les no journey is impossible. To the Underworld then, since
King Eurystheus places this task upon me."

Mount Taenarus, located in Greece, furnished an approach to
the Underworld. The son of Jupiter made his way through a
dark cavern. Suddenly he caught sight of a barking dog. But
what a monster! What teeth! Three horrible mouths! Such is
Cerberus who faithfully guards the gates of his master, named
Pluto. "This is the last labor," our hero thought to himself.
"The gods aid the brave!" With all his might he dragged
Cerberus to the light of day.

From the walls of the city Eurystheus saw the hero dragging
the monster by his tail. He again hid in his vase. He shouted in
a loud voice, "Your twelve labors are completed! Good-bye!"
And Hercules no longer served the cowardly king. After many
other labors, which he voluntarily undertook, he died and
finally became a god himself.

As our author Seneca says, "The journey to the stars from the
earth is not easy."

Latin often has two forms for Greek names. The queen of the
Amazons is called either *Hippolytē-ēs* or *Hippolyta-ae*. We
have used the Latin form *Hippolyta,* but the English name is
"Hippolyte."

Questions

1 Cujus zōnam Herculī imperat Eurystheus? Hippolytae.
2 Ubī latet Eurystheus ex Herculis timōre? In vāse immēnsō,
in vāse grandī, in vāse magnō.
   (Although *ubī* has not appeared yet in the programmed
   materials, it has been fairly frequent in the reader.)
3 Quod mōnstrum Herculēs in Hispāniā vincit? Gēryonem.

4 Ex quō metallō facta sunt māla quae dracō custōdit? Ex aurō.
5 Quod animal jānuam Plūtōnis custōdit? Cerberus.
6 Quot capita gerit Cerberus? Tria.
7 Quod membrum Cerberī tenet Herculēs? Caudam.
8 Cui nōn placet hoc opus forte? Eurystheō.
9 Quis post mortem suam deus fit? Herculēs.

Readings

1 People do not look at the teeth of a horse which is given to them. (St. Jerome, *Ep. ad Ephes*, proem.)
   The passive sounds clumsy in English. Our expression is, "Don't look a gift horse in the mouth."

2 The mind and character and planning and feeling of the state lie in its laws. (Cicero, *Pro Cl.* 53.146)

3 Thus passes the glory of the world. (Anon.)

4 A life without learning is like an image of death. (Dionysius Cato)

5 Silence is a sign of wisdom and talkativeness is a sign of stupidity. (Petrus Alphonsus)

6 Poverty is the sister of an honest mind. (Petronius, 84)
   If you are honest, you will be poor.

7 Ignorance of the law excuses no one. (Legal)

8 In case of extreme necessity all things are in common. (Legal)

9 Fear of God is the beginning of wisdom. (*Job* 28.28)

10 What is sleep except the image of chilly death? (Ovid, *Am.* 2.9.41)

11 From the faults of someone else the wise man corrects his own fault. (Publilius Syrus)

12 In an evil situation a good frame of mind is half of the evil. (Plautus, *Ps.* 458)

> In an evil situation, a confident attitude will by itself take you halfway towards overcoming the evil.

13 Reason is the leader of life. (Latin equivalent of the motto of Phi Beta Kappa)

14 The force of conscience is great. (Cicero, *Pro Mil.* 23.61; *Tusc.* 2.17.40)

15 The safety of the people is the supreme law. (Legal)

16 Every evil begins in the name of the Lord. (Anon.)

> Fanatics believe that they are in the right.

17 The friendship of the king is not an ideal possession. (Med.)

18 Life without learning is death and the burial of a living man. (Seneca, *Ep.* 82.3)

19 The voice of the people is the voice of God. (Commonplace)

20 With love of virtue. (Motto)

> Or, "With love of courage."

21 Rome is the capital of the world. (Adapted from Lucan, *Ph.* 2.655)

22 Disaster is the opportunity for bravery. (Seneca, *De Prov.* 4.6)

23 Anger is the beginning of insanity. (Adapted from Ennius, *F.* 438, quoted by Cicero, *Tusc.* 4.23.52)

24 For the freedom of my country. (Motto)

25 Music is medicine for a sad mind. (Anon.)

26 An enemy outside the city is the greatest bond of concord inside the city. (Anon.)

People cooperate when they are confronted with an outside threat.

27 Talk is an indicator of the mind. (Med.)

28 All art is an imitation of nature. (Seneca, *Ep.* 65.3)

29 Love of money increases as much as money itself increases. (Juvenal, 14.139)

30 For the fear of death is dispelled by music. (Censorinus, *Lib. De Nat.* 12)

31 Against the evil of death there is no medicine in the gardens. (Med.)
   This was a good excuse for the ancient doctors; if the patient was fated to die, the doctors were powerless.

32 Wine is the mirror of the mind. (Anon.)

33 Experience, the great teacher of life, teaches us much. (Cicero, *Rab. Post.* 9)

34 The head of a dove, the tail of a scorpion.
(St. Bernard?)
   Said of someone who appears kind but is actually cruel.

35 A man without money is an image of death. (Anon.)

36 Speech is given to all, wisdom of mind to few.
(Anon.)

37 The miser is good toward no one, but toward himself he is always worst of all. (Varro, *Sent.* 156 in edition of Chappius)

38 For a good many people, the cause of their poverty is honesty. (Curtius, *Am.* 4.1.20)

39 Enough eloquence, little wisdom. (Sallust, *Cat.* 5.4)

40 A long stay of no guest is pleasant. (Anon.)

41 The person who owes does not like the threshold of the person he owes money to. (Publilius Syrus)

If someone owes you money, you are not going to see him at your house very often.

42 Honors are the rewards for virtue. (School motto)

43 Times pass in the manner of running water. (Med.)

44 A friend is the half of one's soul. (Austin, *Confess.* 4 cap.)

45 There are as many superstitions in the world as there are stars in the sky. (Burton)

Note that the construction changes: *mundī* is a genitive modifying *superstitiōnēs*, while *caelō* is ablative showing "place where."

Poems

Africanus has millions, but still he pursues legacies./Fortune gives too much to many, enough to nobody. (Martial 12.10.1)

In dealing with large sums of money, the Romans used the word *sestertium.* which was originally the contracted genitive plural of *sestertius.* The *sestertius* was a small coin; a laboring man earned about four of them a day. In using large sums of money, as here, the Romans used *mīliēns* ("a thousand times"); the question is, a thousand times what? The unit understood was a hundred thousand *sesterces,* so that the fortune of Africanus amounts to a thousand times a hundred thousand *sesterces,* or one million. The reference to "pursuing" is the common practice in Rome of paying attention to people in order to be left money in their wills.

He is sad, pale, does not sleep, eats nothing, is feverish./Calliodorus is not sick however: he is in love. (Parkhurst, 1573)

The students' attention has been called to the fact that *trīstātur* is a deponent verb, although the term "deponent" is not used.

This quotation is from an obscure author named John Parkhurst (1512-1575), Bishop of Norwich, who wrote a number of poems in imitation of Martial. One reason that such poems from Renaissance and modern times are included in this reader is to give the student some idea of the continuity and permanence of the Latin language.

Seven cities compete about the origin of the famous Homer: Smyrna, Rhodes, Colophon, Salamis, Chios, Argos, and Athens. (Anon.)

Additional Readings

Multae terricolīs linguae, caelestibus ūna.
There are many languages for those who live on earth, for those who live in heaven only one. (Anon.)

Multae īnsidiae sunt bonīs.
There are many ambushes for good people. (Cicero, *Sest.* 48.102)

Nōn omnibus omnia.
Not all things for all people. (Anon.)

Sānīs sunt omnia sāna.
For the healthy all things are healthy. (Med.)

Stat sua cuique diēs; breve et irreparābile tempus omnibus est vītae.
His own day of death awaits each person; the span of life is short and irretrievable for everyone. (Vergil, *A.* 10.467)

Annuit coeptīs.
He approves of our beginnings. (Seal of the United States)
   Based upon Vergil, *G.* 1.40 and A. 9.625, *Audācibus annue coeptīs.*

Custōdītur perīculō quod placet multīs.
What is pleasing to many people is guarded with danger. (Med.)

Multa petentibus dēsunt multa.
Many things are lacking for those who seek many things.
(Anon.)

Vigilantibus, nōn dormientibus, jūra subveniunt.
The laws help those who are watchful and not those who are
sleeping. (Legal)

> Ignorance of the law is no excuse. One must be vigilant
> to protect one's rights.

Suus rēx rēginae placet, sua cuique spōnsa spōnsō.
Her own king pleases a queen, and his own fiancée pleases every
man who is engaged to be married. (Anon., expanded on the
model of Plautus, *Stich.* 133)

Dat bene, dat multum, quī dat cum mūnere vultum.
The person gives graciously and gives much, who gives a kind
expression with a gift. (Med.)

Impedit ingenium formōsae cūra puellae.
Anxiety for a pretty girl hinders the mind. (Med.)

UNIT 23

Filmstrip

The Roman Empire[1]

The teacher is referred to the *Guide to Filmstrip Series RŌMA ANTĪQUA* for additional notes on this filmstrip. It is recommended that the story be read only if the filmstrip has already been viewed by the students.

1. On this map are written the names of countries which today occupy the borders of the Roman Empire.

2. Here is shown the Roman Empire in the second century A.D., when it expanded to its maximum under Trajan.

3. The Empire was guarded by rivers, mountains, and seas. When these natural defences were lacking, the Romans built camps and walls.

4. In the Main Forum Trajan is celebrating a triumph, having added Dacia, Arabia, Mesopotamia, and Armenia as provinces to the Empire.

5. In the city of Rome, along with Roman citizens, are found foreigners, both Greeks and barbarians, who were merchants, soldiers, and philosophers.

6. In the faraway provinces Roman armies bravely and faithfully defended the boundaries of the Empire.

7. In all parts of the Empire were found roads, over which the edicts of the Emperor were carried.

8. This rider, who carries either public or private messages, is called a *tabellārius*.

9. Without well-built roads administration is not easy. Such roads aid everyone: messengers, soldiers, merchants, and travellers.

10. To Rome, from Egypt, Britain, Gaul, Syria, India, and Spain

---

[1] The numbering system of the reader begins with the first text frame, unlike the filmstrip guide which includes title and credit frames.

flowed clothing, wine, slaves, jewels, statues, oil, vases, grain, and things of this kind.

11. For example, in this picture there are Greek vases, on which are painted pictures. Greek vases were beautiful and utilitarian.

12. Secretaries (clerks) who served in the administration were both free men and slaves.

13. Spacious buildings made of marble made Rome magnificent.

14. In all the arts, even in architecture, the Romans owed much to the Greeks.

15. The population required a large supply of water, which flowed from the mountains in aqueducts. These aqueducts are usually built under ground, but when they cross a valley or a low place they are put on arches.

16. This aqueduct stands in a plain near Rome. Built by the Emperor Claudius it was called the Claudian Aqueduct.

17. Arches were useful to the Romans; in them statues were often placed.

18. Many statues are to be seen in Rome. This is a statue of a Roman Emperor.

19. These books contain the works of Roman authors. Marcus Aurelius, a Roman Emperor, and Plutarch, who was a Greek, wrote in the Greek language.

20. There were two kinds of Roman books: the *cōdex* was like a modern book; here is another kind, which is called a *volūmen*.

21. The whole world served the Roman Emperor.

22. But this rule was light and not heavy. In many ways the inhabitants of the provinces looked after their own affairs. Because of this they remained loyal.

23. Even barbarians who served the government bravely and faithfully were often made Roman citizens.

24. Under Roman law all citizens in all parts of the Empire were equal.

25. There were many illustrious leaders of the state. This is a bust of Gaius Julius Caesar, who conquered Gaul. After he was made dictator, he was assassinated.

26. The heir of the Deified Julius was Augustus, under whom flourished the poets Horace, Ovid, and Vergil.

27. Hadrian changed the plans of Trajan and no longer extended but contracted the boundaries of the Empire.

28. Marcus Aurelius, a noted philosopher, served the country faithfully on the borders of the Empire. A man of peace, he

spent his life in warfare.

29. In the fifth century the barbarians conquered the western part of the Empire. But the memory of Rome did not die. Roman ways and Roman skills live today.

30. For example, Latin did not die. In our schools many students read Latin.

31. The languages of many European countries are derived from Latin. English has also borrowed many words.

32. The year has twelve months and a month has thirty days. This system of the months was discovered by the planning and effort of Gaius Julius Caesar.

33. The English names of the months are taken from the Roman calendar. As an indication of respect, the names of the months *Quīntīlis* and *Sextīlis* were changed and called "July" and "August."

34. The Romans often considered matters from a practical point of view. They carried on business, waged wars, and constructed buildings, aqueducts, and roads. But the Roman people surpassed other nations in the following ways: they ruled many different races under just laws and they gave the world the *Pāx Rōmāna*.

35. In the eastern part of the Empire, in the sixth century, the Emperor Justinian compiled the body of Roman Law.

36. Even today many countries of Europe are governed by this system of law.

37. This colony, located in Germany and called *Augusta Trēvirōrum*, followed the pattern of a military camp.

38. Our public buildings are often like Roman ones. For example, here is the United States Supreme Court.

39. There remains in Europe, Asia, and Africa Roman bridges, basilicas, and amphitheaters. Some are even now in use. But Roman ideas, arts, and knowledge still live in our lives.

40. People who live today are like these ancient Romans in their customs, laws, and systems of justice.

41. The Roman government and ours are made up of three parts, involving men who pass the laws, those who interpret the laws, and those who administer them.

42. Rome was the ancient head of the Christian religion.

43. This is the story of Rome, the eternal city, of Latin, the language which never died, and of the Empire, which always remains in the mind of man.

Questions

1 Cujus sub rēgnō maximē patet Imperium Rōmānum? Trajānī sub rēgnō.

2 Ā quibus dēfenduntur fīnēs Imperiī? Ā mīlitibus Rōmānīs, ab exercitibus.

> (But not *flūminibus, montibus, maribus, castrīs, mūrīs,* for which the question would have been *Quibus.*)

3 Quibus beneficium dant viae bonae? Omnibus; viātōribus, tabellāriīs, mīlitibus, mercātōribus.

4 Suntne scrībae servī an līberī? Servī vel līberī.

> (Freeman and slave worked together in almost every field of activity.)

5 Quis aedificat Aquam Claudiam? Imperātor Claudius.

6 Quid est genus librī quī similis librīs hodiernīs est? Cōdex.

7 Ā quō capta est Gallia? Ā Gajō Jūliō Caesare.

8 Ā quō fīnēs Imperiī contractī sunt? Ab Imperātōre Hadriānō.

9 Ā quō imperātōre scrīptus est liber philosophiae? Ā Mārcō Aurēliō.

10 Quotō saeculō Jūstiniānus corpus jūris scrībit? Saeculō Sextō.

Readings

1 Piety is the foundation of all the virtues. (Cicero, *Pro Planc.* 29)

2 The cure for injuries is forgetting about them. (Publilius Syrus)

> The students may be influenced by the English word "oblivion" and think that the cure for injuries is unconsciousness. The saying means that if someone injures us, the remedy for our own distress is to forget (and forgive) the injury.

3 A woman faithless to her husband is a shipwreck of one's fortune. (Anon.)

4 A friend of all is a friend of nobody. (Anon.)

> The person who is equally friendly with everybody has no friends in particular.

5 Rome, goddess of earth and of people,
to whom nothing is equal and nothing is second.
(Martial, 12.8.1-2)
> Rome is not only first, but nothing could even be considered second to her.

6 Jupiter laughs at the lies of lovers. (Lygdamus, 3.6.49)
> It is expected that lovers are not going to be strictly truthful.

7 Repetition is the mother of studies. (Anon.)

8 A great number of books distracts the mind. (Seneca, adapted; apparently based on *Ep.* 2.3, *Distringit librōrum multitūdō.*)
> Too much reading, like too much of anything else, can be a vice; many people who could be productive writers or scholars are not, because they spend all their time reading.

9 Who gives quickly gives twice. (Alciatus?)

10 Everything is full of foolish people. (Cicero, *Ad Fam.* 9.22.4)

11 Reason is the mistress and queen of all. (Cicero, *Tusc.* 2.21.47)

12 Truth out of the mouths of little children. (Anon.)

13 Necessity is the mother of the arts. (Anon.)
> "Necessity is the mother of invention."

14 The whole world is the temple of the immortal gods. (Adapted from Seneca, *De Ben.* 7.7.3)

15 History is the witness of time, the light of truth, the life of memory, the teacher of life, the messenger of antiquity. (Cicero, *Or.* 2.36)

16 Strife among the citizens is an opportunity for the enemy. (Publilius Syrus)

17 All the possessions of friends are in common. (Adapted from Cicero, *Off.* 1.16.51)

In the original, Cicero is quoting a Greek proverb and uses indirect statement.

18 The roots of literary study are bitter, but the fruits are sweet. (Ascribed to Cato by Diomedes; Putsch, p. 289)

It is hard work to learn a language but the rewards are great.

19 In the country of the blind, the one-eyed is king. (Anon.)

20 Night is the best nurse of cares. (Ovid, *Met.* 8.81-2)

Sleep induces forgetfulness of cares.

21 The root of all evil is greed. (*I Timothy* 6.10)

22 A heavy task is lightened by the hands of many. (Anon.)

"Many hands make light work."

23 Who is the good man?/He who keeps the decrees of the Senate, who observes laws and justice. (Horace, *Ep.* 1.16.40)

24 Nothing in human affairs is carried out without the will of a god. (Nepos, 20.4.4)

25 Delay is the best remedy for anger. (Seneca, *De Ira.* 2.28.8)

When you are angry, count to ten before doing anything.

26 The fool does not receive the words of wisdom. (Anon.)

27 Flattery is always the companion of good fortune. (Veleius Paterculus, 2.102)

Magnus often seems to be similar to the English word "good" rather than "large," as here, and in the expression *Maximum remedium* above, where the natural English expression seems to be "the best remedy."

28 Discord between the classes is poison in a city. (Anon.)

In Rome, there were three *ōrdinēs:* the patricians, the knights, and the common people.

As more difficult sentences are introduced, a literal translation becomes more and more unsatisfactory. "Discord *between* the classes" sounds better than "discord *of* the classes." The students should now be sophisticated enough to understand that there is no one-to-one correspondence, that while a genitive may frequently be translated "of," the word in the genitive may be linked to the word it modifies by other devices, as in the sentence above.

29 The appearances of things are deceptive. (Seneca, *De Ben.* 4.34)

Exceptionally observant students may question the use of a fifth declension noun in the plural. The answer is that *rēs* and *diēs* are the only nouns in all literary periods which regularly have *all* the plural forms. Some fifth declension nouns do have plurals in the nominative and accusative cases. This is another interesting example of "holes in the paradigm."

30 Death is the gateway to life. (Anon.)
Only by dying do we achieve immortal life.

31 All the chorus of the writers loves the woods and flees the cities. (Horace, *Ep.* 2.2.77)

32 The safety of the state is placed in its laws. (Cicero, *In Verr.* 2.1.4)

33 Those who see the faults of others do not see their own faults. (Anon.)

34 The cross is the anchor of life. (Anon.)

35 The gifts of the gods are not always gifts. (Anon.)
What appears to be an advantage may turn out to be a disadvantage; for example, physical beauty may turn out to be a handicap.

36 Flattery, the perpetual evil for kings. (Curtius Rufus, 8.17)

37 The word of God remains forever. (*I Peter* 1.23)

38 Great affairs are carried on not by strength or speed or swiftness of the body, but by plan, authority, and judgment. (Cicero, *Cato Maj.* 17)

39 Tears have the weight of a voice. (Ovid, *Her.* 3.4)

40 The same remedies do not suit all sick people. (Celsus, *De Remed.* 3.1)

41 Contemplation of nature is food for the mind. (Cicero, *Acad.* 2.127)

42 Names of the stupid always cling to the walls. (Anon.)
   "Fools' names and fools' faces are always seen in public places."

43 A grateful disposition is a unique virtue, not only the greatest one but even the mother of all other virtues. (Cicero, *Planc.* 33)

Poems

The doorways of the master stand closed with good reason;/for they are afraid of the teeth which the hungry people have. (Med.)

> Constant stress must be laid upon the *form* of the Latin which lends point to the original. This form is often lost in translation. In this medieval poem which employs a rhyme scheme (as classical Latin does not), the couplet is given its punch by the internal rhyme between *dentēs* and *ēsurientēs*. Since we are using a classical pronunciation, the medieval rhyme between *causā* and *clausa* is not perfect. At this point, the teacher may wish to expose interested students to the medieval pronunciation.

For death is the nature of mankind, and not a punishment. (Grave inscription)

The good buyer tests wine by its odor, color, and flavor;/the odor is tested by the nose, color by sight, and flavor by the mouth. (Med.)

116

Again, a translation into English loses all the point of the original. Note the internal rhyme of *odōre, colōre, sapōre,* and the rhyme of *sapōre* in the first line with *sapor ōre* in the second line.

Additional Readings

Sunt tria damna domūs: imber, mala fēmina, fūmus.
There are three sources of loss to a home: rain, a bad woman, and smoke. (Med.)

Imāgō animī sermō est: quālis vīta, tālis ōrātiō.
Talk is an image of the mind: as one's life is, so is his conversation. (Pseudo-Seneca, *De Mor.* 72)

Quaedam falsa vērī speciem ferunt.
Certain false things have the appearance of truth. (Seneca, *De Ir.* 2.22.4)

Nec modus aut requiēs, nisi mors, reperītur amōris.
No moderation or rest from love is found except in death. (Ovid, *Met.* 10.377)

Virtūtis comes invidia.
Envy is the companion of virtue. (Motto)

Patientia animī occultās dīvitiās habet.
Patience of the mind has hidden riches. (Publilius Syrus)

Ubi innocēns damnātur, pars patriae exsulat.
Where an innocent person is condemned, part of the fatherland goes into exile. (Publilius Syrus)

In terrā caecōrum monoculus rēx.
In the land of the blind the one-eyed is king. (Med.)

Thēsaurus est mulier malōrum, sī mala est.
If a woman is bad, she is a treasury of evils. (Anon.)
    The implication is that if she is a good woman, she is a treasury of good things.

117

Pecūnia ūna regimen est omnium rērum.
Money alone is the ruler of everything. (Publilius Syrus)

Simile est rēgnum caelōrum thēsaurō abscondito in agrō.
The kingdom of heaven is like a treasure buried in the field.
(*Matthew* 13.44)

Memoria est thēsaurus omnium rērum et custōs.
Memory is the treasury and the guardian of everything. (Anon.)

UNIT 24

History

About the Games

Games in which gladiators fought were extremely pleasing to Romans. To our way of thinking, however, these games were cruel. Man fought against man, man against beast, and beast with other beasts. Through these games the Emperors tried to please the Roman people.

Some gladiators were slaves; others were poor people, who hoped to receive large rewards. But what a life, whose companion is always death! The training of the gladiators was extremely strict. Often a gladiator fought to the death with his friend.

Because these games were given by magistrates or by the Emperors, they were often called *mūnera*.[1] These games occupied a whole day from dawn to dark. How many lives were lost in a single day!

Those who fought with animals were called *bēstiāriī*. This type of contest does not offend us too much, for today many people pursue and kill animals of the forest. The Romans also were accustomed to hunting wild beasts in the woods.

Even the Roman Emperors, when they hunted animals, were in some risk. But often the *bēstiārius* shot arrows from an iron cage against the unhappy beasts with no danger to himself. For example, Emperor Commodus even killed animals with arrows from the royal box. The number of animals that perished in the amphitheater is beyond belief! In one day, as we are told, five thousand animals were killed.

---

[1] *Mūnera* means a person's duty, then the pay received for the duty, then a gift, and finally, as here, games.

119

Uneven contests pleased the cruel populace. Therefore, as Martial tells us, an elephant fought with a bull. In the same way, gladiators fought with different arms. The *rētiāriī*, who carried a net and a trident, fought with those called *secūtōrēs* ("followers") or *mirmillōnēs*, who had helmet, shield, and spear. Often if one gladiator died or was wounded, the victor did not escape from his danger, but had to fight again against a second gladiator. This second gladiator was called the *supposittcius* ("substitute").

Sometimes water was let into the amphitheater. In this way a large lake was formed. In this lake floated boats with sailors and soldiers. This contest was called a *naumachia*.

Below[1] is a poem written by Martial, which praises a certain gladiator, Hermes by name. He was superior in three kinds of fighting. First, he fought as a *vēles*, who used a spear. Then he also was a *rētiārius*, fighting with net and trident. Finally he was also an *andābata*, who fought while riding a horse and was almost blind because he wore a helmet which covered his eyes. Hermes was also a teacher of other gladiators.

This section on the gladiatorial games was put into the reader after careful consideration. Too often only the virtues of the Romans have been presented, leaving the students with a picture of an impossibly puritanical nation. While the qualities of *pietās, gravitās,* and *sevēritās* have been heavily stressed, it was thought desirable to at least acquaint the students with the barbarous gladiatorial games. We have not glossed over the facts and we have tried not to be sensational.

Questions

1 Quī lūdōs populō Rōmānō dant? Imperātōrēs, magistrātūs.
2 Quālia sunt haec mūnera, nostrā sententiā? Crūdēlia.
3 Quō locō cum lūdōs spectant sedent imperātōrēs? In pulvīnārī, in amphitheātrō.
4 Quōcum, ut dīcit Mārtiālis, pūgnat taurus? Cum elephantō.
5 Quibus īnstrūmentīs pūgnat rētiārius? Rētī et tridente.

---

[1] Among the poems at the end of the Unit.

6 Contrā quem saepe pūgnat gladiātor victor? Contrā secundum gladiātōrem, contrā suppositīcium.

7 In quō lūdō pūgnant nautae? In naumachiā.

8 Quem gladiātōrem laudat Mārtiālis? Hermem.

9 Quōs docet Hermēs gladiātor? Aliōs gladiātōrēs.

The poem in which Martial mentions the fight between bull and elephant may be of interest to the students.

> Quod pius et supplex elephās tē, Caesar, adōrat
>   hic modo quī taurō metuendus erat,
> nōn facit hoc jussus, nūllōque docente magistrō;
>   crēde mihī, nostrum sentit et ille deum.

Because the devout elephant kneeled before you, O Caesar, and worshipped you,
the one who just recently was so fearsome to the bull,
he did not do this on command, and there was no trainer coaching him;
believe me, he knows that you are our god.

If the students read this poem, they will need to know that *erat* shows past time and that *crēde* is an imperative. The gerundive *metuendus* can be handled as an adjective, "fearsome."

The poem apparently refers to an incident in which an elephant had defeated a bull in combat in the amphitheater. The elephant had then gone to the *pulvīnar* and knelt before the Emperor Domitian, here called "Caesar." Martial says that the animal did this of his own free will, without orders, because he knew what all the Romans knew, that Domitian was a god. Any one familiar with the training of animals knows that the elephant must have been well coached in this trick and went to the royal box upon receiving a secret signal from his trainer.

Readings

1 Those who remove friendship from life seem to take the sun from the world. (Cicero, *De Am.* 23.47)

2 Seven hours sleep is enough for young and old. (Med.)

121

3 Sweet is love of country, sweet it is to see one's own family. (Anon.)

4 Not because things are difficult are we not bold; but because we are not bold, things are difficult. (Seneca, *Ep.* 104)

5 To err is human. (Anon.)

6 You are holding an eel by the tail. (Anon.)

7 It is the function of art to conceal art. (Anon.)
   The true artist makes the performance appear easy.

8 Everybody wants to know everything, but they do not want to learn. (Med.)

9 Neither smelling bad nor smelling good is pleasing to me. (Ausonius, *Ep.* 125)
   He disapproves both of people who are not clean and of those who use perfume.

10 To be in love and keep one's senses is a thing which is hardly given to a god. (Publilius Syrus)
   The poet is talking about the romance of the gods in Greek and Roman mythology.

11 It is pleasant to play the fool at the proper time and place. (Horace, *O.* 4.12.28)

12 Money does not know how to change an incorrupt nature. (Med.)

13 No one ought to be a witness in his own case. (Legal)

14 The man is wicked who knows how to receive a benefit and does not know how to give one. (Plautus, *Pers.* 762)

15 When a woman cries, she is trying to deceive. (Med.)

16 Who asks in a timid fashion is teaching the person he asks to refuse. (Seneca, *Ph.* 601-2)

17 To hold one's tongue is a very great virtue.
(Anon.)

18 The ability to love and be wise at the same time is not given to Jupiter himself. (Anon.)

19 Happy is he who dares to defend bravely that which he loves. (Med.)

20 Just as a field, however fertile, cannot be fruitful without cultivation, so the mind cannot be productive without education. (Cicero, *Tusc.* 2.13)

21 No one, except an innocent person, is accustomed to being optimistic in difficult circumstances.
(Publilius Syrus)

22 Working is praying. (Motto of Benedictine order)

23 The first law of nature is to love one's parents. (Valerius Maximus, 5.4.7)

24 It is hard to make a joke with a sad heart. (Lygdamus, 3.6.34)
    The first two books of Tibullus are followed by a third, formerly attributed to Tibullus and now ascribed as above.

25 It is foolishness to seek justice from the unjust. (Plautus, *Amph.* 36)

26 If God is for us, who is against us? (*Romans* 8.31)

27 A person who wants to do evil always finds reason. (Publilius Syrus)
    While *nōn numquam* means "sometimes," *numquam nōn* means "always."

28 It is not permitted to know everything. (Horace, *O.* 4.4.22)

29 Whom Fortune wishes to destroy she makes foolish. (Publilius Syrus)

What may seem like bad luck is actually the result of our own foolish actions; if Lady Luck has anything to do with it, she can only be the one who makes us foolish.

30 It is a mistake to believe everything, it is a mistake to believe nothing. (Pseudo-Seneca, *De Mor.* 77)

31 It is difficult to keep moderation in everything. (St. Jerome, *Ep.* 108.20)

32 While there is life in a sick person, there is said to be hope. (Cicero, *Ad. Att.* 9.10)

33 It is hard to fly without wings. (Anon.)

34 It is human to love, it is human to forgive. (Plautus, *Merc.* 319)

35 All wish to know; no one wishes to pay the price. (Juvenal, 7.157)
   There are various readings for this line, including *Nō'sse* for *scīre,* and *velint* for *volunt.*

36 Who is silent appears to give consent. (Legal)

37 These are the principles of law: to lead a decent life, not to harm another, to give to each his own. (Justinian, 1.1.3)

38 For it is a bad thing to marry and a bad thing not to marry. (Valerius, 7.7)

39 The king ought not to be under the influence of men but under the influence of God and the law, because the law makes the king. (Bracton?)

40 It is dishonest to conceal dishonesty. (Anon.)

41 It is dangerous both to believe and not to believe. (Phaedrus, 3.1.10)

42 No one can escape either death or love. (Publilius Syrus)

43 The cat likes fish but does not want to touch the river. (Med.)

44 To weep is a certain pleasure. (Ovid, *Tr.* 4.4.37)
>Or, "There is a certain kind of pleasure in weeping."

45 Drunkenness takes away your character, your money, and your reputation. (Med.)

46 Not to feel one's misfortunes is not human, and not to endure them is not manly. (Seneca, *Dial.* 11.17.2)
>*Hominis* modifies *sentīre*, and *virī* modifies *ferre.*

47˙ Who wants to beat a dog, easily finds a stick. (Anon.)
>If you wish to punish someone, it is easy to find a reason.

48 Knowing the laws is not remembering their words, but rather their force and power. (Anon.)

49 To read and not understand is just like not reading. (Anon.)

50 It is the duty of the judge to explain the law, not to make it. (Legal)
>The judge does not make the law but rather administers it.
>*Jūdicis* modifies the infinitive *dīcere.*

51 It is one thing to conceal, and something else to be quiet. (Legal)
>It is permissible not to admit something, if not asked, but it is wrong to falsify when asked.

52 To pretend stupidity at the right time is the highest sort of prudence. (Anon.)

Poems

Zoilus, you who are so carefully dressed in clothes with a long nap, laugh at my clothes which are so threadbare./They're threadbare, all right, but at least they're mine. (Martial 2.58)

Hermes, warlike pleasure of this generation,
trained in every kind of arms,
both fighter and teacher,
throws his own school of gladiators into trembling confusion,
whom Helius fears, but he fears Hermes alone,
for whom Advolans falls, but only before Hermes,
Hermes taught to conquer but not to kill,
Hermes his own substitute,
source of riches for ticket-sellers,
a concern and worry of the gladiator women,
haughty in his warlike spear,
threatening with the triton symbolic of Neptune,
fearful with his drooping helmet,
the glory of every kind of fighting,
Hermes who stands alone and is unexcelled in three kinds of
    fighting. (Martial 5.24)

    Students will be able to understand this poem better if they
have read the article on gladiatorial games in the first part
of this Unit.

    The reference to *casside languida* in line 13 is not clear.
Obviously, it is a third kind of fighting. We have given one
explanation of the *andabata*. Another explanation is that
it refers to the drooping crest of the "Samnite" gladiators,
who also had large shields and short swords. Friedlaender,
the great editor of Martial, thinks the passage may be
corrupt.

Who writes distichs wants to please the reader, I believe, with
his brevity./But, tell me, what good is brevity if there is a whole
book of it? (Martial, 8.29)

Greatest censor and chief of chiefs,
although Rome owes you so many triumphs,
so many temples rising, so many temples being reborn,
so many spectacles, so many gods, so many cities—
Rome owes more to you because she is now chaste.
(Martial, 6.4)

    A full explanation of the references in this poem is given
in the student's reader.

From this point on, some of the poems in the reader are difficult. They require some knowledge of Roman culture (most of
which is explained in the notes), and they introduce (again,
with explanations) structures that the students have not met in
the programmed materials. Each teacher must decide whether
his classes can profit from reading these poems. Perhaps they
would interest only the top students. Teachers with students
of high ability may prefer to concentrate more on the poems
than on any other part of the reader. Again, the teacher is free
to take advantage of the flexibility of the *Artēs Latīnae* program.

Additional Readings

Tempus rērum imperātor.
Time is the ruler of everything. (Family motto)

Inquiētam nōbīs vītam facit mortis metus.
Fear of death makes life unquiet for us. (Burton)

Temeritās est flōrentis aetātis, prūdentia senēscentis.
Rashness belongs to flowering youth and prudence to those
growing old. (Cicero, *Cat. Maj.* 6.20)

Ex parvīs saepe magnārum mōmenta rērum pendent.
Often actions of great importance depend upon small beginnings. (Anon.)

Paucōrum improbitās ūniversa est calamitās.
Wickedness of a few people is a catastrophe for all. (Publilius
Syrus)

Mors malōrum fīnis est, nec saevitia ultrā fāta prōcēdit.
Death is the end of evils, and cruelty does not go beyond death.
(Anon.)
    Here, *fāta* is used in the sense of "death."

Cattus amat piscēs sed nōn vult tingere plantās.
The cat likes fish but does not want to wet his feet. (Med.)

Dūrum est negāre, superior cum supplicat.
It is hard to say no, when one's superior asks. (Publilius Syrus)

Beneficia quī dare nescit injūstē petit.
Who does not know how to give benefits seeks them unjustly.
(Publilius Syrus)
>It is wrong to ask favors if you do not expect to repay them.

Ēnumerāre omnēs fātōrum viās longum est.
It is a long task to count all the ways of fate. (Seneca, *Ep.* 91.12)

Prīmus est deōrum cultus deōs crēdere.
The first step in worshipping the gods is to believe in the gods. (Seneca, *Ep.* 95.50)

Multī sunt quī scīre volunt sed discere nōlunt.
There are many who want to know but do not want to learn. (Med.)

UNIT 25

Story

About the Eye of Night

There are many who know nothing of the Alps or the Mediterranean, but all of us, unless blind, can see in the sky the mountains and "seas" of our moon.

But in these seas there is no water. The moon is a world without water, without air, without life; in truth a dead world where no one lives, nothing flourishes, nothing grows.

There are seven hundred places on the moon, both seas and mountains, which have names. These names are given without any particular reason. For example, in the Oceanus Procellarum there are no storms. No one in the Mare Crisium is sick to the point of death. How much security is there in the Mare Serenitatis? But without doubt the Mare Frigoris contains no heat!

What we call a "sea" on the moon is really a plain. In the Mare Imbrium landed the first rocket ship, sent by the Russians. In the Mare Crisium an American ship, which sent pictures back to earth, made a soft landing.

But the face of our moon shows us not only "seas" but also mountains. These mountains in some ways are like the mountains of the earth, and in other ways they are unlike. There are many "craters," which are similar to our Mount Vesuvius or Mount Aetna. But the origin of our Mount Vesuvius or Aetna is known without doubt: molten rock flowing from a subterranean source created such mountains. The top part of these mountains is called a "crater" because its opening is similar in appearance to the ancient domestic instrument in which wine was mixed with water.

But the origin of the "craters" of the moon is a matter still under dispute. There are as many opinions as there are astronomers. Perhaps their origin is like that of Vesuvius; perhaps they were made from large meteors falling with great speed from the heavens. However, to us who look at the moon at night these craters are very pleasing. The largest mountain of the moon is called "Copernicus."

In Latin the word *satelles* means an inferior who accompanies his superior. Today by the English word "satellite" we mean a heavenly body such as our moon which always accompanies another planet. Scientists also call a satellite a rocket which flies in a similar way around our earth through the heavens or even one which makes the journey to the moon.

Why do we give Latin names to the places on the moon? For many centuries the language of scientists was Latin. And today those who discover new flowers give them names in Latin.[1]

You ought to examine carefully this map which describes the moon. Perhaps you do not know the word *palūs* ("swamp"). A swamp is a low place, like a lake, which has shallow water. Frogs and mosquitoes live in swamps, but in the Palus Somnii how many frogs are there? There are as many frogs there as there are fish in the Mare Hiemis or sailors in the Mare Autumni.

In the above account, the place names of the lunar features have not been translated. The following is a list of the meaning of these names, along with those added on the map. These names are written without macrons because they are now English names.

Oceanus Procellarum: Sea of Storms
Mare Crisium: Sea of Crises
Mare Serenitatis: Sea of Serenity
Mare Frigoris: Sea of Cold
Mare Imbrium: Sea of Showers

---

[1] One of the most popular books on the moon (*Survey of the Moon* by Patrick Moore, New York, 1963) has this to say (p. 65): "Latin is still the universal language, and therefore astronomers use Latin rather than English names."

Palus Somnii: Swamp of Dream(s)
Mare Hiemis: Sea of Winter
Mare Autumni: Sea of Autumn
Mare Fecunditatis: Sea of Fertility
Mare Humorum: Sea of Dampness
Sinus Iridum: Bay of Rainbows
Lacus Mortis: Lake of Death
Mare Nectaris: Sea of Nectar
Sinus Roris: Bay of Dew
Mare Spumans: Foaming Sea
Mare Tranquillitatis: Sea of Tranquillity
Mare Undarum: Sea of Waves

Questions

1 Quid est "Oculus Noctis"? Lūna.
2 Quanta aqua in maribus lūnae est? Nūlla, nihil aquae.
   (The teacher may wish to anticipate the programmed materials by introducing the construction, *nihil aquae*, at this
   point.)
3 Ex quō factī sunt montēs Vesuvius et Aetna? Ex igneō
lapide, ex saxō fluentī.
4 Quid est orīgō crātērārum lūnae? Sub jūdice līs est;
crātērae factae sunt ex lapidibus magnīs ē caelō cadentibus;
ē saxō fluentī.
5 Quī sunt virī doctī quī faciem lūnae spectant? Astrologī.
6 Quae sunt nōmina quīnque locōrum plānōrum quōs nōs
"maria" vocāmus? Mare Crisium, Ōceanus Procellārum, Mare
Serēnitātis, Mare Frīgoris, Mare Imbrium, Palūs Somniī, Mare
Hiemis, Mare Autumnī.
7 Quāliter nōminantur hodiē flōrēs plantaeque? Latīnē.
8 In quō īnstrūmentō miscēbātur vīnum cum aquā? In crātērā.

Readings

1 While we teach, we learn. (Sergius, Keil, 4.486.11)

2 You surpass the snail in slowness. (Plautus, *Poen.* 3.1.29)

3 We give praise of virtue to necessity. (Quintilian, 1.8.14)

We praise someone for his virtue when he is only doing what is necessary.

4 I judge you from your own mouth. (Anon.)

5 I neither have, nor want, nor care. (Motto)

6 You are insanely looking for water in the middle of the river. (Propertius, 1.9.16)
   Latin frequently uses an adjective where English would use an adverb: "You, an insane person, are looking . . ."

7 While I breathe, I hope. (Motto of Viscount Dillon)
   "Where there is life, there is hope."

8 We all, while we are well, willingly give good advice to the sick. (Terence, *And.* 309)

9 You are making an elephant out of a mouse. (Anon.)
   "You are making a mountain out of a molehill."

10 While we flee fate, we foolishly run into the same fate we are trying to avoid. (Buchanan?)

11 Other people's things please us, and our things please other people more. (Publilius Syrus)

12 Riches are the cause of evil. (Anon.)

13 Socrates said, "How many things I do not want!" (Anon.)

14 We all write, learned and unlearned. (Burton)

15 I hear but I keep silent. (Motto of Lord Kesteven)

16 When we are sick, then we are the best. (Pliny the Elder, Book 7?)
   When people are ill, they are more ready to listen to advice.

17 I am fighting with the winds. (Petronius, 83)

18 I am a man; I consider nothing human alien to me. (Terence, *Heaut.* 78)
    Quoted by Cicero in *De Off.* 1.30, with *nihil* in place of *nīl*.

19 Where the laws are strong, there the people can be strong. (Publilius Syrus)

20 My riches are mine; you belong to your riches. (Seneca, *De Vit. Beat.* 22.5)

21 You are in the same boat (as I am). (Anon.)

22 It is foolish to fear what you cannot avoid. (Publilius Syrus)

23 If we believe the Greek poet, sometimes it is pleasant even to take leave of our senses. (Seneca, *De Tran.* 17.10)

24 We easily give advice to other people. (Burton)

25 Serving God is true liberty. (Med.)

26 No one ought to be judge in his own case, because one cannot be both judge and participant. (Legal)

27 The lowly person cannot fall far nor heavily. (Publilius Syrus)

28 To be in control of one's self is the greatest control. (Seneca, *Ep.* 113.24)

29 No one can know everything. (Varro, *R.R.* 2.1.2)

30 To accept a benefit is to sell one's liberty. (Publilius Syrus)

31 The brave person can fall but he cannot yield. (Family motto)

32 To punish a man who is asking for mercy is not courage but cruelty. (Publilius Syrus)

33 Who is able to take clothes away from a person who does not have any clothes? (Plautus, *Asin.* 1.1.79)

34 The fish cannot love the fisherman. (Burton)

35 Lovers cannot judge about beauty. (Burton)

36 The gods sell us everything at the price of our labor. (Anon., quoted by Priscian, Keil, 432.23)

37 It is a youthful fault not to be able to control one's impulses. (Seneca, *Tr.* 259)

38 A good tree cannot bring forth bad fruit nor can a bad tree bring forth good fruit. (*Matthew* 7.18)

39 You are doing something which has been done before. (Plautus, *Pseud.* 261)
    You are sounding trite.

40 We do not flee our vices by changing our location. (Anon.)

41 While we drink, while we ask for garlands, ointments, and girls,/old age creeps up on us undiscovered. (Juvenal, 9.128-9)

42 There certainly is a God, who sees and hears what we do. (Plautus, *Capt.* 2.2)

43 Everyone can take away a man's life, but no one can take away his death. (Seneca, *Phoen.* 152-3)
    This requires two explanations. First, *nēmō nōn* is a strong way of saying "everyone." Second, to the Stoics and the Romans in general, unlike to ourselves, suicide was an honorable means of death. Seneca, therefore, means that it is possible to kill a man, but it is not possible to prevent a brave man from committing suicide.

44 Fortune can take away your wealth, but not your personality. (Seneca, *Med.* 175)
    An unabridged dictionary lists many meanings for *animus,*

anima, and *mēns.* Generally speaking, *mēns* is mental capacity, whereas *animus* is personality, and *anima* is the soul.

Poems

Remember that these poems are more difficult than the material traditionally met in first-year Latin texts.

Your beard is white and your hair is black./You cannot dye your beard (this is the reason) and you can, Olus, dye your hair. (Martial, 4.36)

> At this time the Romans were generally clean-shaven; *barba* means the stubble or bristle (which he can't dye, because the dye would stain his face as well as the stubble).

I give to you a mock naval battle and you give me a book of epigrams./Marcus, I think that you ought to go floating with your book (in my naval battle). (Martial, 1.5)

> Martial puts these words into the mouth of Domitian. Marcus is Martial's first name. The lines express the insolence of Martial's sending a book of poems in repayment for a naval battle. Such a "gift" might conceivably lead Domitian, says Martial in jest, to throw both Martial and his book into the water.

I reply little to you who always ask so much,/not because you ask for much but because you ask for foolish things. (Owen)

I praise the true God, I assemble the people, I call the clergy together,/I weep for the dead, I dispel pestilence, and I adorn festival days. (Inscription on church bell)

I summon the living, I mourn for the dead, I destroy the lightning. (Inscription on church bell)

You repair the stable a little late when the thief is already taking away the bulls;/the father instructs his son a little late when the guest is already seeking his house. (Med.)

Cinna, you are always chattering into everybody's ear,/even when you are talking about something which it is permitted to talk about with a whole crowd of people listening in./You laugh into people's ears, you complain, argue, weep,/you sing into people's ears, pass judgments, keep quiet, shout,/and this disease has seated itself so deeply in you,/Cinna, that you often praise Caesar in people's ears. (Martial, 1.89)

> The construction of *adeō*, *ut*, and the subjunctive to show result is pointed out to the student. The student is also reminded that *quereris* is a deponent verb. (The teacher should remember that the students do not have the passive or deponent use of *-ris* in *Latin: Level One*.)

Word Game

You take (or, you took) from things that were forbidden. Adam is thirsty, Eve is thirsty, we are thirsty. (Anon.)

> This is a palindrome, which reads the same backward or forward. The long quantities are not marked because they would spoil the joke.

Many teachers will not care to spend time on these oddities. Perhaps it would be well to let some of the class try them and ascertain their reaction. Most of the ones we have included were well known in the schools of Germany and Hungary. It is apparent, of course, that the ability to read Latin and the ability to solve word puzzles like this are different skills. And yet the fun of playing with words in sentences like these may well be some preparation for the study of poetry, where the author uses language in unusual ways.

Additional Readings

Nōn metuit mortem quī scit contemnere vītam.
The person does not fear death who knows how to despise life. (Dionysius Cato, 4.26)

> When one realizes how empty and futile life is, then death does not seem so bad.

Sī poēma loquēns pictūra est, pictūra tacitum poēma esse dēbet.
If a poem is a talking picture, then a picture ought to be a silent poem. (Anon.)

Inhonesta victōria est suōs vincere.
It is a dishonorable victory to overcome one's own people. (Pseudo-Seneca, *De Mor.* 68)

Solet esse in dubiīs prō cōnsiliō temeritās.
In dubious circumstances rashness is often taken for planning. (Publilius Syrus)

Beneficia plūra recipit quī scit reddere.
The person receives more benefits who knows how to give them. (Publilius Syrus)

Nōn lātrat frūstrā vetulus canis et sine causā,
verbaque prūdentum pondus habēre solent.
An old dog does not bark in vain and without cause,
and the words of the wise usually have weight. (Med.)

Dolōris medicīnam ā philosophiā petō.
I seek from philosophy a remedy for my grief. (Cicero, *Acad.* 1.3.11)

Habēs amīcōs quia amīcus ipse es.
You have friends because you yourself are friendly. (Pliny, *Paneg.* 85)

Crēdō quia absurdum.
I believe because it is absurd. (Tertullian, *De Cor. Chr.* 2.5)
> One does not need faith to believe what can be intellectually proven, but rather what cannot be proven.

Sed cūncta timēmus amantēs.
But we lovers fear everything. (Anon.)

UNIT 26

Three Stories

About the Lame Spartan

The Spartans were brave soldiers as our story shows.

A certain Spartan soldier was lame. Certain people laughed at him. "Look! Here is a lame soldier who wants to go to war!" He replied,[1] "But my idea is to fight, not to run away."

Questions

1 Quāliter currere poterat noster mīles Spartānus? Male, nōn celeriter, lentē.
2 Quāliter pūgnāre volēbat? Bene, fortiter, nōn īgnāvē.
   (The verb *volēbat* here means "intended.")

How Will You Learn?

Son: Father, why do bulls have long tails, but pigs have short ones?
Father (reading his newspaper): I don't know, son; why do you ask?
Son: I just want to know. Tell me, how do elephants sleep?
Father: What do you mean?
Son: Do they sleep standing up or lying down?
Father: I really don't know.
Son: Who was the best Roman emperor? Who was the worst?
Father: I don't care about the Romans. They're all dead.
Son: When will the next American ship be sent to the moon?
Father: The moon? The scientists don't keep me informed about this.
Son: I have some other questions, father. Shall I ask them or keep quiet?

---

[1] Note the historical present *respondet.*

138

Father: Ask, my dear son, always ask! How can you learn unless you ask?

1 Quid legēbat pater? Ācta diurna.
2 Quāliter respondēbat quaestiōnibus fīliī suī? Male, stultē.
3 Quālia respōnsa dat pater? Mala, stulta.

Suitable Grounds for Divorce

A certain person (appearing) before a judge said, "I want a divorce."
The magistrate replied, "Why do you wish to divorce your wife? Have you grounds?"
"Yes, I have."
"What fault does she have? How does she prepare the food?"
"She's a good cook," replied the other.
"Does she bother you with her nagging?"
"No, sir. She is kind by nature. Her disposition pleases me."
"What's the fault, then?"
"She keeps a goat in our bedroom."
"But what about the goat? Does he hurt you?"
"He doesn't hurt me, but he smells bad. I can't stand the smell."
"But if the odor is bad, why don't you open the window?"
"Me? Open the window? If I did this, all my birds will fly out of the bedroom!"

1 Quid petēbat quīdam ā jūdice? Dīvortium.
2 Quālem causam dīvortiī, ut ipse ait, habēbat? Jūstam, bonam, aptam.
3 Quālem cēnam parābat uxor quam repudiāre volēbat? Bonam.
4 Quō locō dormiēbat uxōris caper? In cubiculō.
5 Quae animālia quoque in cubiculō habitābant? Avēs.

Readings

1 We will be thirsty in the middle of the water. (Ovid, *M*. 9.761)

2 I will not therefore estimate men according to their fortune but according to their character; each person gives himself his character but chance assigns us our status in life. (Macrobius, *Sat.* 1.11.10)

3 I am what you will be. (Tombstone inscription)
   Namely, dead.

4 If things are bad now, they will not be this way at some time in the future. (Horace, *O.* 2.10.17-8)

5 Anger will give strength. (Seneca, *Tr.* 1.681)

6 The Roman people who once gave/military command, the fasces, legions, and everything, now/restrain themselves and they only anxiously hope for two things,/bread and circuses. (Juvenal, 10.74-81)
   The word *circēnsēs* is an adjective; the full phrase in this context would be *lūdōs circēnsēs. Tantum* is an adverbial accusative meaning "only."

7 Today no one, tomorrow the mightiest.
   (Anon.)

8 You will conquer by hard work. (Family motto)

9 After three days a fish and a guest often start to go bad. (Med.)

10 If one blind man leads another, both fall into the pitfall. (Anon.)
   "The blind leading the blind."

11 Thou shalt love the Lord thy God with all thy heart, and thy neighbor as thyself. (*Luke* 10.27)

12 The wise man will command his emotions, the foolish man will obey them. (Publilius Syrus)

13 If you say abusive things to others, you will hear abusive things in return. (Plautus, *Pseud.* 1173)

14 There will be vices as long as there are men. (Tacitus, *Hist.* 4.74)

15 Today, not tomorrow. (Motto)

16 In the sweat of thy brow shalt thou eat thy bread. (*Genesis* 3.19)

17 Great is truth and it will prevail. (Anon.)

18 Who says what he wants will hear what he does not want. (Adapted from Terence, *And.* 920)
    The *quī* is not in Terence.

19 I will keep the faith. (Family motto)

20 The just will flourish as the palm tree.
   (*Psalms* 91.2)

21 If you are happy with your fortune, you will live wisely. (Anon.)

22 No friend will come to riches which have been lost. (Ovid, *T.* 1.9.10)
    If you have lost your money, you will not have any visitors.

23 Cato against the world. (Anon.)
    This refers to Marcus Porcius Cato Uticensis; his last name (*agnōmen*) was posthumously given because of his suicide at Utica (in Africa) when he was defeated by Julius Caesar. Like Pompey, Cato was a symbol in later years for those who wished to express mild opposition to the Imperial administration. The virtues of his life were much lauded and somewhat exaggerated. The expression is used of someone who takes up a cause which he feels to be righteous, even though it is unsupported by public opinion.

24 The blind man is the leader for the blind. (Med.)

25 Our king was Elizabeth, now our queen is James. (Anon.)
    Elizabeth I was a powerful ruler. Her successor, James I

(the son of Mary, Queen of Scots, and before his assumption of the English throne, James VI of Scotland), was a weak and unpopular king.

26 Who loves danger will die in danger. (Anon.)

27 He who drinks this water will be cured if he adds faith. (Seen at famous spas)
    The students may need an explanation of the European spas and the procedure of "taking the waters" which were supposed to have a curative effect.

28 God will provide for me. (Family motto)

29 It will not always be summer. (Anon.)

30 Where will I not climb? (Family motto)

31 What does not happen today will happen tomorrow. (Petronius, 45)

32 The diligent farmer plants trees whose fruit he will never see: will not a great man plant laws, institutions, and a state? (Cicero, *Tusc.* 1.14.31)

33 You will perceive innermost thoughts by external actions. (Med.)

34 A fox often finds a good path through the vines. (Med.)
    A smart person can solve problems that confound others.

35 He (lies in the grave) today, I (will lie in one) tomorrow. (Grave inscription)

36 Everything which is yours will be of no advantage to you after your death. (Anon.)

37 A brave bear is disturbed by a swarm of flies;
    Ulysses was not able to conquer Troy by himself. (Med.)
        By cooperation, we accomplish much.

Poems

Little soul, fleeting, kindly,
guest and companion of my body,
what places will you go to now?
Pale, inflexible, naked little soul,
you will not continue to joke as you usually do.

> This poem was written by the Emperor Hadrian when he
> thought his death was near. The diminutives suggest the
> frailty of the bond between body and soul. As with many
> poems, it is difficult to say precisely what he meant by
> calling the soul *vagula* or *blandula*. The adjectives *palli-*
> *dula*, *rigida*, and *nūdula* may well be taken to modify *loca*;
> these places are gloomy, oppressive, and bare. When such
> ambiguity occurs in poetry, the poet is generally trying to
> convey both meanings at once.

My name was Primus, while life remained in me./Cheated of
the light of day, I rest below the realms of heaven./Now my
rest is secure, now there is no danger of life. (Grave inscription)

> The belief that death is a respite from the trials of life is
> commonly expressed in grave inscriptions.

Asia and Europe cover the younger Pompeys,/but the soil of
Africa covers Pompey the Great, if indeed any soil covers him
at all./What is so strange if this family is scattered over the
whole world?/Such a ruin could not lie in one place. (Martial,
5.74)

In times of prosperity there are many friends counted;
but if fortune disappears, there will be no friend at all.
(Med.)

Aemilianus, you will always be poor, if you are poor now.
Riches are given to none except the rich. (Martial 5.81)

> Martial cynically says that people now give money only to
> the wealthy, so that they can receive money in return. It
> may be well to tell the students that the Latin term *pauper*
> was not ordinarily used in the sense of our word "pauper."

143

Martial described himself as being a *pauper*, but he belonged to the equestrian order. To be a knight, or *eques*, meant that he must have had at least 400,000 sesterces.

I was poor, I am, and I always will be (I think) poor.
Mennus, the poet tells you the reason:
"You will always be poor if you are poor, Aemilianus;
riches are given today only to the rich." (Parkhurst)

You are going to marry Fausta? Alexius, she is not going to marry you;/but she is going to marry your money. (Parkhurst)

Word Games

Considerable help is given the students on these next two readings, with successive stages of hints.

The *Ō* is over the *be*. The *quid* is over the *est*. The *tuae* is over the *biae*. If you use the Latin preposition *super* (meaning "over"), the following results: *Ō superbe, quid superest tuae superbiae?* This means, "O proud one, what is left of thy pride?" The English example is "John Underwood, Andover, Massachusetts."

The next *lūsus* is of a different kind. There are three syllables *ra*, three syllables *ram*, and two syllables *ī*. If we put *ter* ("three") before the *ra* and *ram*, and *bis* ("twice") after the *ī*, we get the following: *Terra es et in terram ībis*, meaning, "Dirt thou art and to dirt thou shalt return."

Additional Readings

Nōn est in mundō dīves quī dīcit, "Abundō."
There is no rich man in the world who says, "I have enough."
(Med.)

Deum nōn vidēs, tamen Deum agnōscis ex operibus ejus.
You do not see God, but you recognize God from his works.
(Cicero, *Tusc.* 1.70)

Tōtō caelō, ut dīcitur, errātis.
As the saying goes, you are wandering over the entire sky. (St. Jerome, *C. Faust.* 20.6)

Inimīcitiam atque amīcitiam in frontem prōmptam gerō.
I carry my hostility and friendship in my frank countenance. (Ennius, *F.* 106)

In flammam flammās, in mare fundis aquās.
You are pouring fire into fire, and water into the ocean. (Ovid, *Am.* 3.2.34)

Quī nescit dissimulāre nescit rēgnāre.
Who does not know how to pretend does not know how to rule. (Anon.)

Quī potest trānsferre amōrem potest dēpōnere.
The person who can transfer his affections can lay them aside altogether. (Publilius Syrus)

Quod nātūra negat tollere nēmō potest.
What nature denies no one can take away. (Translation of Aesop)
    You can not lose what you do not have.

UNIT 27

Poem

The House That Jack Built

Only the translation of the last stanza is needed, since the others can be reconstructed from it. Here is the nursery rhyme version:

> This is the farmer sowing the corn,
> That kept the cock that crowed in the morn,
> That waked the priest all shaven and shorn,
> That married the man all tattered and torn,
> That kissed the maiden all forlorn,
> That milked the cow with the crumpled horn,
> That tossed the dog,
> That worried the cat,
> That killed the rat,
> That ate the malt,
> That lay in the house that Jack built.

We have used the word *mūs* to translate "rat" since the Romans didn't have rats.

The following is a literal translation.

First line
> Jack built this house.

Last stanza
> Here is the farmer sowing seed,
> who owns the rooster, crowing daily,
> who woke the priest shaven and shorn
> who married the ragged man
> who kissed the sad unhappy girl
> who milked the cow whose horn was deformed
> who tossed the dog

146

who worried the cat
who killed the mouse
who ate the barley
which lay in Jack's house.

Questions

1 Quō locō jacēbat hordeum? Domī Jacōbī, in aedibus Jacōbī, in aedificiō Jacōbī.
2 Quod animal possidēbat agricola? Gallīnāceum.
3 Quem in mātrimōnium dūxit vir inops? Virginem miseram et maestam.
4 Ā quō clērus cottīdiē excitātus est? Ā gallīnāceō.
5 Quem necat fēlēs? Mūrem.
6 Cui nocuit canis? Fēlī.
7 Quālia cornua gerit vacca? Prāva, mala.

The teacher should observe the shift from the present perfective tense to the historical present.

Filmstrip

The Life of Julius Caesar[1]

The teacher is referred to the *Guide to Filmstrip Series RŌMA ANTĪQUA* for additional notes on this filmstrip. The EBE sound film, "Julius Caesar: The Rise of the Roman Empire," may be used to supplement this filmstrip.

1. Here is Caesar! Is he a tyrant or a man of the greatest leniency?
2. Gaius Julius Caesar killed many thousands of men in war, but often prided himself on his "leniency."
3. Modern rulers often take to themselves the name of "Caesar." But people who act in a tyrannical fashion are also called "Caesar."

---

[1] The numbering system of the reader begins with the first text frame, unlike the filmstrip guide which includes title and credit frames.

4. When he was alive, because of his popularity with the people he was called "Father of His Country."

5. But he was killed by the senators. After his death he was made one of the gods.

6. In the consulship of Caesar, in 59 B.C. the territory of the Republic stretched this far.

7. Rome was the capital of the world. In the middle of the city was the Forum Romanum.

8. When Caesar was a young man, the Roman Senate ruled the civilized world both by its prestige and by its power.

9. The senatorial order was elected from noble families or from "new men," who, from a humble background, became outstanding in public life by their own achievements.

10. There were two other ranks, the equestrian and the plebeian. The *equitēs* were men who possessed a sufficient amount of money. For the most part, the *plēbs* consisted of poor men, without prestige, and almost without hope. At this time, money alone ruled Rome.

11. From this inequality grew discord, hatred, and civil war.

12. Therefore, there were in the state two kinds of men . . .

13. . . . a few rich men, either senators or knights, who ruled the state . . .

14. . . . and many poor people, who were fed partly at public expense.

15. The cause of this poverty was the employment of slaves, who were often captured in war.

16. Because of this great number of slaves, it was difficult for free men to find work. In the first place, the slaves worked on the great plantations, which were called *lātifundia*. Now slave labor and not free labor was the basis of Roman agriculture. Small farmers, who possessed few or no slaves, were unable to earn a living from agriculture.

17. Many poor people sold their farms and migrated to the City . . .

18. . . . where they lived in dirty tenements along with many other poor people. How could a farmer work in the City?

19. The officials tried to please the people with many games and processions. But poverty is not satisfied by spectacles; many people desired a change.

20. Many think to themselves, "We will be able to get these luxuries by means of violence."

148

21. In such dangerous times the young Julius was educated. In school, the boys gave their attention to the art of the orator.

22. Nobles who aid the common people, and in turn are aided by them, áre called *Populārēs*, of which the opposite is *Optimātēs*. Caesar, even as a young man, sought the favor of the people.

23. He gave many benefits to both the rich and the poor. The *Optimātēs* feared his growing power.

24. He entered upon the *cursus honōrum*. He was a strict but just judge.

25. The magistrates who were called *aedīlēs* were accustomed to putting on shows. As aedile, Caesar produced lavish games, both with his colleague, Marcus Crassus, and by himself.

26. In 59 B.C. he was elected consul with Marcus Calpurnius Bibulus, whom the *Optimātēs* supported.

27. Caesar was an eloquent orator. His ability gained him many friends and very many enemies.

28. But Bibulus was an incompetent, who, giving up hope about his position, soon retired to his house and did nothing in his whole consulship except to announce evil omens. Caesar ruled by himself. But there were two other powerful men, of whom one was . . .

29. . . . Crassus, who, beyond all his contemporaries, possessed both riches and ambition. The other was . . .

30. . . . Pompey, called the "Great" because of his victories, who won the favor of the *Optimātēs*.

31. This triumvirate divided the world among themselves. Pompey took an army to Spain, and Crassus, one to Asia.

32. Against the wishes of the *Optimātēs*, Caesar took Gaul for himself with the assistance of Pompey and Crassus.

33. Gaul, still unconquered, was next to the boundaries of the Republic. The Romans feared the Gauls for many years.

34. "All Gaul is divided into three parts, one of which is inhabited by the Belgians, the second by the Aquitanians, and the third by those who call themselves Celts but whom we call Gauls," wrote Caesar in his Commentaries.

35. After Caesar had waged war for six years, Vercingetorix, a leader of the Gauls, started an insurrection, and soon all Gaul was in arms against Caesar.

36. It was difficult to overcome Vercingetorix. Here Caesar is planning strategy with his officers.

37. In skill and discipline the Romans far surpassed the uncivilized Gauls.

38. After a bitter and difficult war, Vercingetorix was captured and later led in Caesar's triumph. Finally he was put to death in prison.

39. Caesar is writing to his friends, "I have waged war in this region for ten years. Now I want to return to the City and seek a second consulship."

40. But there was a great difficulty which he is explaining to his officer. "If I lead my legions across the boundaries of my province, I will be acting against the will of the Senate. But if I discharge them, I will be helpless."

41. The society of the Triumvirate was now broken. Crassus was dead in Asia; Pompey with the *Optimātēs* was opposed to Caesar.

42. Caesar crossed the Rubicon River (which was the boundary of his province) and journeyed to Rome. Pompey with the two consuls and many *Optimātēs* fled to Greece. Caesar waged civil war against Pompey for five years and finally emerged as victor.

43. Caesar celebrated five triumphs because of his victories.

44. Often elected consul, he made himself dictator in perpetuity. He was not a king, but alone he held the *imperium*.

45. But he was a wise and kind leader. He showed leniency even to his enemies.

46. Through his edicts he extended Roman civilization to the distant provinces. By such works he established the foundation of the Roman Empire.

47. He extended the franchise to many races.

48. The *Populārēs* loved Caesar. But envy increased among the *Optimātēs*. Sixty senators and knights devised a dangerous plan. They formed a conspiracy and . . .

49. . . . on the Ides of March they assassinated him at the meeting of the Senate.

50. But this crime was futile. Octavian, afterwards called "Augustus," avenged the death of Caesar and himself became the *prīnceps*.

51. For five centuries the state was ruled by the Emperors. Here we see Trajan who was one of the so-called "Good Emperors."

52. Men of many nations became Roman citizens. Rome made one city what had formerly been a world.

Questions

1 Quī Jūlium Caesarem necāvērunt? Senātōrēs.
(Actually there were some *equitēs* involved in the plot; see Eutropius 6.25.)
2 Ex quō ōrdine erat Caesar ipse? Ex ōrdine senātōriō.
3 Quot ōrdinēs in rē pūblicā Rōmānā erant? Trēs.
4 Quid erat ōrdō summus? Senātōrius. Medius? Equester.
Īmus? Plēbejus.
5 Cujus artem discēbat Caesar juvenis? Ōrātōris, ōrātiōnis.
(Either the art of an orator or the art of oratory is correct.)
6 Quī magistrātūs mūnera vel lūdōs populō dabant?
Aedīlēs.
(In Imperial times the Emperor usually presented the exhibitions.)
7 Quōs duōs collēgās habēbat in triumvirātū Caesar?
Crassum Pompejumque.
8 Quem collēgam habēbat in cōnsulātū suō? Mārcum Calpurnium Bibulum.
9 Quī ex Caesare suffragium accipiunt? Multī, multae gentēs, multī populī.
10 Ā quō vindicāta est mors Caesaris? Ab Octāviānō.

Readings

1 Nature has given us the seed of knowledge; she has not given us knowledge. (Seneca, *Ep.* 120.3)
Nature gives us native intelligence, but we have to do the learning ourselves.

2 He has taken the thunderbolt from the sky and the sceptre from the tyrants. (Turgot)
This is an inscription on a bust of Benjamin Franklin, referring to his discovery of the nature of lightning, the accompanying invention of the lightning rod, and his part in the American Revolution. The line is apparently an echo from Manilius' book on astronomy (1.104): *Ēripuitque Jovī fulmen vīrēsque tonandī* ("He has taken the thunderbolt from Jupiter and his power to make thunder"). This reference is to the philosopher Epicurus who tried to free men from superstition.

151

3 I am a Roman king and above grammar. (King Sigismund the First?)

> Sigismund was the name of three kings of Poland. The one referred to here lived from 1467 to 1548. By calling himself a *rēx Rōmānus*, he meant that he viewed himself as a spiritual heir of Roman emperors, even if he sometimes made mistakes in his Latin.

4 There has been no great genius without a mixture of madness. (Seneca, *Dial.* 9.17.10)

5 He falls into the pit which he dug himself. (Anon.)

6 The river which has passed by will never be called back, and the hour which has passed can never return. (Ovid, *A. A.* 3.64-5)

7 I am not as foolish as I was before. (Ovid, *Am.* 3.11.32)

8 Fortune is fickle: she quickly demands the return of what she has given. (Publilius Syrus)

9 He adorned *everything* which he touched. (Oliver Goldsmith's epitaph written by Samuel Johnson)

> Here again, the figure of litotes (*nūllum nōn*) is strong in Latin, but it is impossible to translate this literally into English since we cannot say, "He did not adorn nothing which he touched."

10 God caused the storm and they are scattered. (Motto on medal commemorating defeat of Spanish Armada)

11 We hate a person whom we have hurt. (Anon.)

12 Broad is the gate and wide the road which leads to destruction, and there are many who enter through it. (*Matthew* 7.13)

13 The person who perishes through courage does not die. (Plautus, *Capt.* 690)

14 The conquered person weeps, the victor has died.
(Anon.)

>This is a reference to a war in which the results were
>disastrous for both sides, but even more so for the con-
>queror than the conquered.

15 God has given, God has taken away. (*Job* 1.21)

16 Not even Hercules can do anything against two people.
(Anon.)

17 The dead person has not perished, but just gone away.
(Grave inscription)

18 The person who has planted something will care for it.
(T. Roosevelt)

>This seems to refer to Theodore Roosevelt's interest in
>conservation.

19 Fortune takes away the least from you when she has given
you the least. (Anon.)

20 Cupid hates the lazy. (Ovid, *A. A.* 2.229)
"Faint heart ne'er won fair lady."

21 Slaves are human beings and they drink one kind of milk
just like ourselves, even if a bad fate has oppressed them.
(Petronius, *Sat.* 71.1)

>This sentence contains "bad Latin." We have included it
>for two reasons. One is the thought expressed in the first
>century A.D. that slaves are men like ourselves. Slavery
>was frequently defended on the grounds that those en-
>slaved were not really human beings.

>The second reason refers to the word *lac*. In earlier times,
>*lac* had been a neuter; here it is masculine; it also occurs
>as masculine a century later in Apuleius. The form *fātus*,
>a masculine, in place of the neuter *fātum*, is also attested
>in a fifth century historian. This illustrates the beginning
>of a tendency which resulted in the disappearance of the
>neuter in all the Romance languages.

Exposing the student to too much "bad Latin" (that is, Latin which uses non-classical forms) is not desirable, but occasional illustrations like this one are dramatic proof that languages in fact do change.

22 Gloomy people hate the person who is cheerful, and those who are jolly hate the gloomy one,/the quick hate the person who sits around, and those who are lazy hate an active and busy person. (Horace, *Ep.* 1.18.89)

23 The city which captured the whole world is now captured. (Anon.)
Attributed to St. Jerome.

24 You say what pertains neither to heaven nor to earth. (Petronius, 44)

25 I am much obliged to old age, which has increased my desire for talk and removed the desire for drink and food. (Cicero, *Cato Maj.* 14.46)

26 Money has made no one rich. (Seneca, *Ep.* 119.9)
Real riches consist of something besides material possessions.

27 Who laughed last laughed best. (Anon.)

28 When there has been a fire for a long time, the smoke is never lacking. (Anon.)
"Where there's smoke, there's fire."

29 Many know many things, no one knows everything. (Anon.)

30 The Lord has given. (Motto of Lord Herries)

31 Who has begun has half the job done. (Horace, *Ep.* 1.2.40)
"Well begun is half done."

32 Happy is he who knows the rural divinities. (Vergil, *G.* 2.493)

A farmer who worships the traditional, ancient gods of the country is a happy person.

33 Whoever has spared evil people harms good people. (Anon.)

When evil-doers are not punished, they are free to inflict their evil deeds upon innocent people again.

34 True love does not know how to have moderation. (Propertius, 3.6.30)

35 Through no fortune can you avoid death. (Med.)

36 What no one knows almost does not occur. (Apuleius, *M.* 10.211)

37 Happy is he who is able to learn the reason for things
and put all fears and implacable fate
under his feet. (Vergil, *G.* 2.490-2)

The reference is to Epicurus who tried to free men from superstition.

38 Who spares the rod hates his child. (*Proverbs* 13.24)

39 Adam, the first man, damned the centuries with the fruit. (Med.)

40 Blessed is death which opens the door to blessed life. (Burton)

41 To the lions with the Christians! (Tertullian, *Apol.* 40.2)

The accusative *Christiānōs* is the object of an understood verb, such as "throw."

42 This was true, is true, and will be true: a person seeks someone who is like himself. (Med.)

Poems

I, when I was still a young man, made this monument for myself. (Grave inscription)

I lived faithfully without strife and without complaint of anyone in fidelity./Those who knew me well praised my life./After an honest life I have come to my eternal home. (Grave inscription)

> Students may need to be reminded that the person who is supposed to be speaking on the tombstone did not necessarily write the inscription.

Stranger, what I say is short; stand and read./Here is the unlovely grave of a lovely woman./The parents named her name Claudia./She loved her husband with all her heart./She bore two sons. One of them/ she leaves on earth, and has placed the other underground./She was a woman of charming speech, but also of graceful carriage./She kept her home; she spun her wool. I have spoken. Depart. (Grave inscription, *C.I.L.* 1.2.1211)

> This inscription is used in the EBE sound film, *Ingenium Rōmae* (identical to the EBE film, "The Spirit of Rome," but with a Latin soundtrack). There are three imperatives which the students have not yet had: *astā, perlege,* and *abī.* It should also be pointed out to the students that *locat* in line 6 is the historical use of the present (#2) tense; she is not *now* placing the second son under the ground, but she *has* placed him underground.

> This inscription was written about 150 B.C. The archaic spelling has been "normalized"; for example, the first two lines actually read:
> Hospes, quod deico paullum est, asta et pellege.
> Heic est sepulchrum hau pulcrum pulcrai feminae.

Either Asia, Europe, or Africa covers the great Pompeys.
What a family it was which lies in the whole world!
(Seneca, *Ep.* 13)

> It is believed by some that these lines were not written by Seneca. A similar poem by Martial appears in Unit 26.

Afer, when you returned safely from African tribes,/I tried for five days to say "Hello!"/People said, "He is not at leisure," or, "He's sleeping," to me when I came back twice

and three times./Well, this is enough. Afer, you don't want
to have me say hello to you. Goodbye. (Martial 9.6)

> The verb *vult* frequently has the meaning of "try," as here.
> Notice how difficult it is to translate the poem. *Avē* and
> *valē* both mean "Be healthy" but the first was said in
> Martial's time as a greeting, and the other as a farewell.
> *Nōn vīs avēre* means "You don't want to be said 'Hello'
> to," and so Martial says *"Valē"* ("Be healthy" or "Good-
> bye"). The additional twist in this is that *valē* was the call
> given to people when they died, as a sign of farewell.
> From now on, Afer is not going to figure very prominently
> in Martial's affairs.

Bassus bought some cloaks for ten thousand sesterces,
Tyrian cloaks of the finest color. He made money on the deal.
"Did he buy them then so cheap?" you ask.
No; he's not going to pay for them. (Martial, 8.10)

On A Powdered Face

When she puts on her powder, Sertoria puts on her face.
When she loses her powder, she also loses her face.
(Seneca, Poem 46)

> There is some question about whether these poems were
> written by Seneca.

Galla wants to see all the verses which I have written./I will
send them if, in repayment for the books, she will give me her
lips. (Sannazaro)

> One of the points here is the resemblance between *librīs*
> (books) and *labra* (lips).

Aelius was seized with a disease and got well.
But when he saw the doctor Simplicius, he died. (Parkhurst)

Word Game

This poem is not only Latin but Italian. It was written by
Mattia Butturini (1752-1817). It is essential to point out to

the students that while Italian does resemble Latin in many
ways, this *lūsus* is exceptional. Furthermore, when this poem
is presented to Latin students in Italy, it is necessary to explain
some of the Italian words, which are now rare or poetical.

I salute thee, bountiful Goddess, generous Goddess,
O our glory, O queen of Venice!
In the stormy deadly tempest
thou rulest calmly;
thou hast laid low a thousand fearless bodies in bitter battle.
Because of thee I am not sad, because of thee I do not moan,
because of you I live in peace. Rule, O blessed one!
Rule in prosperity, in holy majesty,
in everlasting splendor, on a golden throne!
Thou calm, peaceful, holy,
kind, save me, love me, and preserve me.

Additional Readings

Nōn omnī diē bene esse potest.
Things do not go well every day. (Anon.)

Sēro serās pōnis stabulō post fūrta latrōnis.
You are putting the bars on the stable (rather) late after the
theft of the robber. (Med.)
  "Locking the barn after the horse is stolen."

Arbor inīqua bonōs nescit prōdūcere frūctūs.
A bad tree does not know how to produce good fruit. (Med.)

Nihil est aliud bene et beātē vīvere nisī honestē et rēctē vīvere.
Living well and happily is nothing except living honestly and
righteously. (Cicero, *Parad.* 15)

Dominus prōvidēbit.
The Lord will provide. (Family motto)

*Sī ad nātūram vīvēs, numquam eris pauper; sī ad opīniōnem,
numquam eris dīves.*

If you live according to nature, you will never be poor; if you live according to your own personal opinion, you will never be rich. (Seneca, *Ep.* 16)

Seneca is referring to spiritual riches.

Doctor erat quālis, tālis fit saepe scholāris.
As the teacher was, so often the scholar becomes. (Med.)

Dē paucīs lignīs numquam fīet bonus ignis.
A good fire will never be made out of a few pieces of wood. (Med.)

UNIT 28

Filmstrip

Roman Architecture[1]

The teacher is referred to the *Guide to Filmstrip Series RŌMA ANTĪQUA* for additional notes on this filmstrip. Unlike the texts of the other filmstrips in the RŌMA ANTĪQUA series, "Roman Architecture" may be used to advantage if the class has examined the two sets of study prints, "Historical Reconstructions of Rome" and "Historical Reconstructions of Pompeii," even though the students may not have worked with the filmstrip itself.

If the teacher and class are particularly interested in archaeology, they can make good use of the other filmstrips and sound films which show the Roman Forum. In discussing the various buildings, a map should be referred to constantly.

1. In the pictures which you will see will be many ruins. With the assistance of an artist these ruined buildings will be restored. For example, in the picture which follows, you will see a view of modern Rome which is well-known, namely . . .

2. . . . the Roman Forum. But except for the triumphal arch which stands on the right, everything has been destroyed.

3. Look! Through the skill of the artist the city is now restored. How different from the last picture!

4. ABOUT ROMAN TEMPLES: The ancient Romans did not have sacred buildings but worshipped the divinities of nature under the open sky. But later they built temples similar to the Greek temples. For the most part nothing remains of these buildings except their foundations. Almost all the Roman temples which exist today belong to the time of the Republic.

---

[1] The numbering system of the reader begins with the first text frame, unlike the filmstrip guide which includes title and credit frames.

5. Here you see a Roman temple. In many ways it is like a Greek temple, but in other ways it is different.

6. In the first place, the Greek temple was placed on a low foundation which is called a "stylobate." In front of the temple was placed an altar which the priests used to sacrifice victims.

7. These are the ruins of the temple of Apollo, which is located in the Forum at Pompeii. Is the foundation high or low?

8. The high Roman foundation is called a *podium*. What is the name of the low Greek foundation? (Stylobate.) The Greek temple was located in a remote spot; the temple of Apollo is in the middle of the Forum.

9. A view of the restored temple. It had this appearance, we believe, in the third century B.C. In Greek fashion, there is an altar before the temple.

10. There were three kinds of columns. The Doric column was austere, the Ionian was graceful, and the Corinthian was ornate and magnificent.

11. What kind of columns does our temple of Apollo have? Are they Doric, Corinthian, or Ionic? (Corinthian.)

12. THE ROMAN FORUM or THE GREAT FORUM: We will return to the Great Forum, which was the heart of the government. Here were triumphal arches and columns, here were sacred temples, and here were public buildings.

13. Here the Roman Forum has been restored. But no human being ever saw this view of the Forum. Buildings of various periods have been mixed together.

14. All tourists who come to Rome go through these ruins. Some of them think, "Did the Roman Empire rise from such miserable ruins as these?"

15. Look! Here is the same Forum as it was (if we can believe our artist) in Imperial times.

16. In the Great Forum there are many large monuments which call to mind the memory of famous leaders. Among these are columns and triumphal arches.

17. On the left stand the columns, on the right the arch of Septimius Severus, built at the beginning of the third century A.D.

18. What is the name of the street which passes under the arch of Septimius? (Sacred Way.) Whose temple is located on the top of the Capitoline Hill? (Temple of Jupiter.)

19. In Greek buildings are found many doorposts, which support lintels. In Roman buildings, however, there were many arches.

20. Vaults were made out of several arches.

21. This was the appearance of the Basilica of Maxentius in the fourth century A.D.

22. Here we see the ruins of the same basilica. As Vergil said, about Hector when he saw him dead and covered with dirt, "How changed from him we knew!" (*Aen.* 2.274)

23. ABOUT THE BASILICA OF MAXENTIUS: In these basilicas, both administrative matters and lawsuits were conducted. The basilica which you saw above was built by the Emperor Maxentius in the fourth century A.D. The interior is unbelievably luxurious. The statue of the Emperor Constantine was a colossal statue, ten times life-size.

24. In this sketch you can see the vaults, arches, and porticos of the Basilica of Maxentius.

25. This is the site of the Circus Maximus, as it appears today.

26. The Romans were great spectators. Three hundred thousand people used to gather in this Circus Maximus to watch the chariot races and other games.

27. At the time of Constantine, the Circus Maximus looked like this. The charioteers used to drive their horses around a low wall called the *spīna*.

28. Who does not know about the Roman Colosseum? Here fifty thousand people used to sit, here man fought with man and man with beast, and here, as the story goes, the Christian martyrs perished. In the Middle Ages there was a song:

> As long as the Colosseum stands, Rome will stand;
> When the Colosseum falls, Rome will fall.
> And when Rome falls, then falls the world.

29. What a magnificent ruin modern tourists can see!

30. Here is the Colosseum as it was in the first century A.D. The colossal statue which can be seen at right is that of the Emperor Nero.

31. Here fifty thousand spectators used to sit. In the middle are the underground chambers where wild beasts were imprisoned.

32. ABOUT THE THEATER: In addition to the gladiatorial shows, there were stage shows, which were plays written for acting on the stage. In the Roman theater, the tragedies for

the most part were acted in Greek, and the comedies in Latin.
33. You are looking at the sketch of a Greek theater, which the Romans used as a model in building. But there were some differences. The Greek theater stood on the side of a hill . . .
34. . . . but the Roman theater was situated on flat ground.
35. At Pompeii there exists today this well-preserved theater. The place where the spectators sat was called the *cavea*.
36. Here you see the same theater restored by our artist. Above the *cavea* is stretched the *vēlārium* (or "awning"), which shades the spectators.
37. ABOUT PRIVATE BUILDINGS: The house which you will see in the next pictures is found in Pompeii. It is ornate and spacious. In the middle of the house is an "atrium." The shape of this building is unusual because there are two atria. In these luxurious homes there was also a "peristyle," that is, a garden around which the house was constructed.
38. The statue is standing in the *impluvium*, which is a receptacle for rainwater in the middle of the atrium. Through the doorway we can see the peristyle.
39. Between the atrium and the peristyle is the *tablīnum* where the father of the house did his reading, his writing, and received his friends.
40. Every part of the house had its own function. The residents slept in the bedroom, washed in the bathroom, and food was prepared in the kitchen.
41. This building, which is in Pompeii, was called a *pistrīnum*. For what purpose was it built?
42. A *pistrīnum* is a shop where grain is ground by mills. These mills are turned by the use of donkeys or slaves. In a *pistrīnum* is often found an oven, where bread is cooked.
43. In this reconstruction you can now see the wood, from which the fire is made. loaves of bread placed on the table. and grain stored in sacks.
44. From such buildings, both public and private, we can understand the glory of Roman civilization. Even in death the Romans sought magnificence. In the next pictures you will see the tomb of a Roman Emperor.
45. ABOUT HADRIAN'S TOMB: The tomb of Hadrian stands across the Tiber River. Is the bridge ancient or modern? You will find out in the next picture.
46. Hadrian, who ruled after Trajan, was one of the "Good

Emperors." The tomb has been preserved through the centuries because it was turned into a fort.

Questions

1 Utrum est fundāmentum humile, stylobata an podium? Stylobata.
2 Quid est nōmen fundāmentī templī Rōmānī? Podium.
3 Quōrum theātra in plānitiē stābant? Rōmānōrum.
4 Cum quō virō Trojānō comparātur Forum hodiernum? Cum Hectore mortuō.

> (The reader is in error here; the filmstrip compares the Basilica of Maxentius, not the Forum, with the dead Hector.)

5 Quid hodiē vidēre possumus in Forō Rōmānō? Aedificia vāstāta, arcum triumphālem.

> (There are many other possible answers to this question.)

6 Quō umbrābantur spectātōrēs in theātrō? Vēlāriō.
7 Quō locō sedēbant spectātōrēs in theātrō? In caveā.
8 Quī molās circumagēbant in pistrīnō? Asinī, servī.
9 Quid coquēbātur in pistrīnī furnō? Pānis.
10 Quō locō pater familiās legēbat, amīcōs accipiēbat? In tablīnō.
11 Cui flūminī proximus est Tumulus Hadriānī? Tiberī.

Readings

1 They despise the thorns when the roses have fallen. (Ovid, *F*. 5.354)

> People will accept unpleasant things when there is something pleasant connected with them, but will then condemn them when the pleasant aspects have been removed.

2 Who accuses himself cannot be accused by someone else. (Publilius Syrus)

3 Not for one's self but for one's country. (Family motto)

4 Laughter without any reason behind it is common in the mouths of the stupid. (Anon.)

5 Gentle in how we do it, firm in what we do. (Motto of Lord Newborough)

The contrast is between *modus* (the method) and *rēs* (the matter which must be taken care of).

6 I have often discovered beautiful people to be the worst, and I have discovered many fine people with unpleasant appearance. (Phaedrus, 3.4.6-7)

7 Conquered Greece captured her savage victor. (Horace, *Ep.* 2.1.156)

The Romans conquered Greece, but the Greeks in turn, through the influence of their superior culture, hellenized the Romans. The result of the Roman victory was the spread of Greek civilization.

8 A good judge condemns what is wrong, but he does not hate it. (Seneca, *De Ira.* 1.16.7)

We speak about hating the sin but not the sinner.

9 Each person ought to stay within his own fortune. (Ovid, *Tr.* 3.4.26)

10 Lovers create dreams for themselves.
(Anon.)

11 The coldness of winter, the riot of spring, the heat
of summer have taken away from the desire for study.
(Med.)

Here are three good reasons for not working.

12 How will he spare either you or me, who does not spare himself? (Med.)

A person who makes excessive demands upon himself can hardly be expected to show consideration for others. The medieval writer intended to write a dactylic hexameter, but *modō* never has the iambic shortening which such forms as *mihī* and *tibī* do.

13 No one is sufficient unto himself; every friend needs a friend. (Med.)

14 It is a wise man who adapts himself to all situations.
(Med.)

15 When a person is sick, he does not do what he persuaded
his sick friend to do when he himself was healthy.
(Med.)

16 Whatever the gods wanted is accomplished. (Ovid, *M.*
8.6.9)

17 The greedy man is good to no one, but toward himself he
is the worst. (Publilius Syrus)

18 There was one world. Columbus said, "There are two."
And there were. (Inscription at Columbus' birthplace)

19 Man is a fragile thing, not lasting for a long time;
   he is therefore similar to the flower which grows in the field.
   (Med.)

20 A person lives an unworthy life, through whose efforts
someone else does not live. (Anon.)

21 Everyone who hates his brother is a murderer. (*I John* 3.15)

22 Friends, I have lost a day. (Suetonius, *T.* 8.1)
   Said by the Emperor Titus when he discovered he had done
   no kind action for anyone on that day.

23 Who helps evil people later has cause for grief. (Phaedrus,
4.18.1)

24 What person in haughty mood the rising sun has seen,
   this person the sinking sun has seen lying prostrate.
   (Seneca, *Th.* 613-14)
        Diēs veniēns, rising sun; *diēs fugiēns*, setting sun.

25 Among evil persons too, virtue has much authority. (Quintilian, *Decl.* 253)
        This is an example of *multum* being used as a noun modi-
        fied by the genitive *auctōritātis*.

26 What I was able to do, I did to perfection. (Motto of Viscount Melville)

27 Whoever owns the ground owns all the way to the heavens. (Legal)
    More literally, "Whose is the soil, his is the property all the way to heaven." *Ūsque* is an intensifier.

28 All things are afraid of the person who is afraid of God; but the person who is not afraid of God is afraid of everything. (Petrus Alphonsus)

29 Who is afraid of all ambushes falls into none. (Publilius Syrus)

30 Done quickly enough if done well enough. (Cato, in *Aul. Gel.* 16.14)

31 When a tree has been blown down, whoever wants the wood collects it. (Anon.)
    In times of misfortune, people try to profit from the situation.

32 Fortune is unrestrained equally in good and in bad. (Laberius?)

33 A watchman stands above, who looks at us and our actions every day. (Anon.)

34 Often one day gives what an entire year has denied. (Med.)
    A person may work on a problem for a long time, and then suddenly have the answer come to him in a flash.

35 Generally people gladly believe that which they want to believe. (Caesar, *B.G.* 3.18.2)

36 Gratitude which is expressed late is an ungrateful kind of gratitude. (Anon.)

37 Wine does that which the waves of the sea do not. (Med.)
    Wine is more dangerous than the ocean. Both wine and

the sea can make a person sick, and can cause him to lose all his possessions, but wine more so than the sea.

We must remember that sailing in ancient and medieval times, even disregarding lack of auxiliary power, was more hazardous than today. Until development of a keel, boats could not beat into the wind and therefore could easily be driven onto the lee shore.

38 Who scorns smaller gifts loses the bigger gifts. (Med.)

Poems

A nut, a donkey, a bell, and a lazy person do nothing without beating;/the first is hard, the second is slow, the third is silent, the fourth stays in bed./As soon as they feel the blow of iron or the elm,/the first one falls from the tree, the second one starts to go, the third one rings, and the fourth one studies. (Med.)

The aggressive business man had stolen away the whole city,/ and no threshold had stayed within its own threshold (that is, no business stayed within its own threshold)./Domitian, you ordered the narrow streets to grow,/and what was just a path has become a road./Now there is no pillar surrounded by chained goblets,/nor is any praetor forced to go in the middle of the mud;/now no razor is blindly drawn in the dense crowd,/ nor does any restaurant, black from smoke, take up the entire street./Barber, innkeeper, cook, and butcher all keep within their own thresholds./Now it's Rome; recently it was just a big shop. (Martial, 7.61)

> The Emperor Domitian, here called by his cognomen of *Germānicus*, had required the shopkeepers to cease to display their wares in the street, and to conduct their business inside the house, that is, *intrā līmina*.

> The poem above is probably too difficult for the average high school class at this point in their learning. Top students, however, should be able to handle it, particularly if they work together.

168

You, who had been the most famous barber in the entire city/
and was afterwards, with the gift of your mistress, made a
knight,/have sought cities of Sicily and the kingdoms near Mt.
Aetna,/Cinnamus, when you fled from the disagreeable judgment of the Forum./Useless as you are, at what skill will you
make bearable these difficult years?/What can this unfortunate
quiet of exile do?/You can't become a rhetorician or a gram-
marian or a master of a school/or a Cynic philosopher or a
Stoic,/nor can you (even) sell your voice and applause in the
Sicilian theatres./What does remain, Cinnamus, is that you
can be a barber again. (Martial, 7.64)

> Freedmen, particularly those who became rich, were looked
> down upon by many of the Roman authors. The point of
> line 9 is that Cinnamus is so stupid and unattractive that
> he can't even earn money by applauding an actor in a
> theater. It was common practice for actors and performers
> to hire people (in English called a "claque") to applaud
> vigorously when they appeared and departed.

While an ant was wandering in the shade of a poplar,
a sticky drop of amber entrapped the tiny creature.
And thus one who, while life remained, had been despised,
by its funeral is now made a precious object. (Martial, 6.15)

> Martial wrote several poems about an insect or small
> animal who became entrapped in some kind of sap. When
> the sap became amber, the animal was immortalized in a
> glorious tomb. The adjective *Phaethontēā* refers to the
> fact that Phaethon's sisters were turned to poplars, and
> wept for his death, at his unhappy adventure with the
> chariot of the sun. The ancients seem to be in error, how-
> ever, in thinking that amber came from the sap of poplars,
> since it comes from that of coniferous trees.

The devil was sick; he was willing to become a good monk.
But when he got well, he remained as he was before. (Med.)

Word Game

I send you a ship lacking bow and stern. (Anon.)

The students are told in the note to look only at the form

169

of *navem,* rather than at its meaning. If we remove the first letter (the bow) and the last letter (the stern), we get *Ave* ("Greetings"). The long quantities are not marked because the /e/ is short in *nāvem* and long in *Avē,* while /a/ is long in *nāvem* and short in *Avē.*

Additional Readings

Amnis et annus abit; semper sapientia stābit.
The stream and the year go by; wisdom will remain forever.
(Med.)

Quidquid sub terrā est, in aprīcum prōferet aetās.
Time will bring out into the sunlight whatever is hidden under the earth. (Horace, *Ep.* 1.6.24)

Contrā malum mortis nōn est medicāmen in hortīs.
Against the evil of death there is no medicine in the gardens.
(Med.)

Īnspicere tamquam in speculum in vītās omnium
jubeo atque ex aliīs sūmere exemplum sibī.
I order him to look into the lives of all as if into a mirror and to take examples from others for himself. (Terence, *Adelph.* 415-6)

Quid faciunt paucī contrā tot mīlia fortēs?
What do so few brave people do against so many thousands?
(Ovid, *Fast.* 2.229)

Nōvimus pectora eōrum: in pāce leōnēs; in proeliō, cervī.
We know their hearts: in time of peace, they are lions; in battle, deer. (Tertullian, *Coro. Mil.* 1)

Ad laetitiam datum est vīnum, nōn ad ēbrietātem.
Wine has been given to man for pleasure and not for drunkenness. (Anon.)

UNIT 29

Story

The Fox Who Lost Her Tail

Once upon a time a fox was caught in a trap, from which she was trying to escape. Suddenly dogs appeared, who attacked the unfortunate creature. After a fierce battle she escaped but with a severe misfortune: through the dogs' biting she had lost her tail. Sadly she returned home.

The other foxes laughed at her. "Where is the adornment and honor of our species?" they asked. "A fox without a tail is like a philosopher without a beard!"

"You are wrong," replied the sly fox, who had conceived of a plan and was pretending happiness. "A missing tail is a gain, not a loss. Now I can run easily; no heavy tail hinders my running. Now gnats don't hide in it. Sharp thorns used to bother this troublesome part of my body. Without a tail I am at last free. O dear friends, if you lay aside your tails, you will be happy. I will personally assist you; I will gladly cut off your tails with my teeth."

"Every fox likes his own tail," replied an old fox. "Before your loss *you* praised your tail above everything else. Now you find fault with that same tail. We know you; we will not remove our tails. If we did this, we will be like you and mourn our loss."

This story is often told about those who make fun of their lost liberty.

Questions

1 Ā quibus cauda vulpis caesa est? Ā canibus.
2 Cujus jactūram plōrābat vulpēs laesa? Caudae suae.

3 Quōcum comparāta est cauda vulpis? Cum barbā philoso-
phī, cum lībertāte āmissā.
4 Quōs dēcipere temptat vulpēs quae caudam āmīserat? So-
dālēs suās, amīcās suās, aliās vulpēs.
5 Quā rē, ut ait vulpēs quae caudam nōn possidēbat, erat
cauda molesta? Erat gravis, in eā latēbant culicēs, spīnae eam
irrītābant.
6 Quid est glōria omnium vulpium? Cauda.
7 Quid laudat quaeque vulpēs? Suam caudam.

Filmstrip

Two Friends[1]

The teacher is referred to the *Guide to Filmstrip Series RŌMA
ANTĪQUA* for additional notes on this filmstrip. The EBE
sound film, "Claudius: Boy of Ancient Rome," tells the same
story as this filmstrip. However, the film, which has an English
soundtrack, is aimed at students in the elementary grades. This
fact should be explained to a more advanced class if the teacher
wishes to use the film.

1. In the second century A.D. Rome was the greatest city in
the world.
2. From Rome were sent commands to distant provinces.
3. Legions brought riches with them from captured provinces.
4. Of such nature and importance was Rome. But the story
which you will read and see is not about the Empire but about
two boys . . .
5. . . . about Claudius, of a famous and noble family . . .
6. . . . and about Vistus, who was a slave in the Claudian family. Between these boys, slave and young master, a firm friendship had been established.
7. These students have met out in the open.
8. For Claudius and Vistus are fellow students, even though
one is free and the other is a slave.
9. According to an old custom, the teacher is Greek, for the
Romans put special emphasis on Greek literature.
10. But above everything else the boys learn Roman values:
seriousness, *pietās*, and strictness.

---

[1]The numbering system of the reader begins with the first text frame, unlike the filmstrip
guide which includes title and credit frames.

11. Alixus, father of Vistus, is a *paedagōgus*, whose job is to accompany the boys to school. Today, on the way home, they meet a band of soldiers.

12. "Someday I too will be a commander of soldiers," think our young friends.

13. Perhaps this will happen to Claudius.

14. But poor Vistus is only dreaming. Slaves can never become officers or even common soldiers.

15. Slaves are thought to be hardly people by many. But masters differ a great deal. Alixus' life is not altogether unhappy. Claudius' father treats his slaves well.

16. "What if I should run away?" thinks Alixus to himself. "This road leads to Gaul, to homeland, and to freedom."

17. The friends do not think about such matters. Master and slave play together without any difference. But when Vistus grows up, he will know the bitterness of slavery.

18. Claudius' parents are old-fashioned. His mother attends to household affairs personally. Now she is helping the servants in the kitchen.

19. The fields produce vegetables which feed the family.

20. The servants are preparing food in the kitchen.

21. When the weather is pleasant, they eat out-of-doors in the peristyle, which is a garden with a wall around it.

22. When wealthy Romans dine, they recline on their elbows. The guest is a foreign trader.

23. Romans added wine to water. Only those of dissipated habits used to drink wine unmixed.

24. Claudius is eating with his sisters, not with the grownups.

25. After dinner the children play together.

26. Among other games there is this board for a game like chess.

27. They try to throw nuts into vases.

28. Late at night Vistus comes secretly to Claudius' bedroom. He does not usually visit his friend so late. "What is it?" says Claudius.

29. "Today my father asked for his freedom."

30. "But he's dreaming! What he wants certainly won't happen."

31. "No, Alixus believes that it will. Your father has freed other slaves."

32. "You won't go with Alixus, will you?"

33. "My duty as a son will compel me to go with him. But I will leave this farm—and you—against my will."

34. After Vistus has gone, Claudius lies awake a long time and thinks.

35. How hard it is to lose a friend!

36. After many days these difficulties are almost forgotten. Nothing is said about the manumission.

37. A chariot is standing without a driver. "Do you want to go a short way with me across the plain?" says Claudius.

38. "How easy it is to drive."

39. Now the horses no longer walk slowly but begin to run.

40. Claudius cannot rein in the frightened horses.

41. Vistus loses his balance, falls . . .

42. . . . and lies lifeless among the rocks.

43. Is he alive or dead?

44. He is alive, but in grave danger. He is seriously ill. Claudius, nursing his friend, keeps watch and grieves.

45. "Vistus was hurt not through an accident but by my fault. What if he should die?"

46. Because his family worships the ancient gods, Claudius goes to the temple of Jupiter Maximus. Here he will offer sacrifices . . .

47. . . . through which his friend will get well again. "O Jupiter Maximus! will you forgive me for my mistake?"

48. Whether through the help of the gods or through the nursing of Claudius, Vistus quickly recovers.

49. But in happiness there is a new trial. "I have some news," says Vistus.

50. "We have been freed by your father. We are no longer slaves but freedmen and we will return to Gaul."

51. But Claudius is much changed as a result of the accident. He doesn't think about his own loss but about his friend's good fortune. "I am happy that you are getting what you want," he says.

52. The day has come when Vistus will leave the Claudian family.

53. All free Roman children wear the *bulla*. Claudius gives his own *bulla* to his friend.

54. "Now that I am wearing this *bulla* I am truly free. Thank you, patron."

55. "I will never forget you."

56. At long last Alixus is returning to his homeland. But Vistus looks back at his beloved household. His heart remains with the Claudian family. "I will come back, patron, I'll come back!"

Questions

1 Cujus familiae erat Vistus servus? Gentis Claudiae.
2 Cujus condiscipulus erat Vistus? Claudiī.
3 Ā quibus cibus parābātur? Ā famulīs, ā servīs.
4 Quō locō famulae cēnam coquēbant? In culīnā.
5 Quid erat locus ubī māter famulās adjuvābat? Culīna.
6 Quālēs erant parentēs Claudiī? Nōbilēs, dīvitēs, benīgnī.
7 Quae animālia currum trahunt? Equī.
8 Cujus culpā Vistus vulnerātus est? Claudiī.
9 Quem ōrāvit? Jovem Optimum Maximum.
10 Prō quō Claudius ōrāvit? Prō Vistō, prō vītā Vistī, prō amīcō, prō salūte sodālis suī.
11 Quid petīvit Alixus ā dominō suō? Manūmissiōnem, lībertātem.
12 Quid erat sīgnum quod gerēbant puerī Rōmānī? Bulla.

At some point the students will need to learn about the system of Roman names. The most usual form was *Mārcus Tullius Cicerō: Mārcus* is the *praenōmen, Tullius* the *nōmen* (the gentile name, name of the family), and *Cicerō* is the *cognōmen*, the name of the particular branch of the family. Within the family Cicero called his son, who had the same name as himself, *Cicerō* and not *Mārcus*.

Readings

1 My friends will forgive me if I stupidly make an error. (Horace, *S.* 1.3.140)

2 Who first draws the sword, his will be the victory. (Livy, 24.38.5)

3 Who has lifted the calf will lift the bull. (Anon.)
Compare a similar expression in Quintilian (1.11.15):
Mīlō quī vitulum assuēverat ferre taurum tulit. This refers

to Milo of Croton, who is said to have started by carrying a young calf; as the calf grew, so did his strength, until at the end he was able to carry a full-sized bull. In recent times this experiment was tried and reported in LIFE magazine; to put it briefly, the bull won.

4 The hungry Greek knows everything; (if you order him) he will go to heaven. (Juvenal, 3.77-8)
   The hungry Greek is obliging and rashly promises a benefactor anything; if you order him to, he will even try to go to heaven. *Jusseris* is not in a *sī* clause, as a speaker of English might expect, but is parenthetical.

5 A lie is thin; the light shines through if you look at it carefully. (Seneca, *Ep.* 79.19)

6 Your things please you, my things please me. (Anon.)

7 In all human affairs, particularly in warfare, fortune is powerful. (Livy, 9.17.3)

8 Black death calls all things to her own jurisdiction. (*Consolatio ad Liviam,* formerly ascribed to Ovid and now believed to have been a work of first century A.D.)

9 The sailor talks about the winds, the plowman about his bulls,/the soldier counts his wounds, and the shepherd counts his sheep. (Propertius, 2.1.43-4)
   Nāvita is an older form of *nauta.*

10 Often a small, despised spark has created a large fire. (Curtius Rufus, 6.3)

11 Many come to their death while they fear fate. (Seneca, *Oed.* 1015-16)
   Fātum in the singular, modified by *suum,* means "one's own death."

12 No man is a good judge in his own affairs. (Med.)

13 Envy, like fire, seeks the highest. (Livy, 8.31)

14 The end tests the undertaking. (Ovid, *Her.* 2.85)

15 Virtue lives after death. (Motto)

16 With courage, not with words. (Motto)

17 The stars influence us but do not compel us.
(Anon.)
> The writer believed in astrology to the extent that he thought the stars do have some influence on our lives, but not an all-powerful one.

18 Who seeks God seeks joy. (Anon.)

19 Socrates was the first to call philosophy down from heaven and set it in the cities and even introduce it into our homes, and make it ask about daily life and customs and good and evil. (Cicero, *Tusc.* 5.4)

20 After many days comes one sunny one. (Lygdamus, 3.6.32)

21 Many courses have created many diseases. (Seneca, *Ep.* 95)
> We speak of a person digging his grave with his teeth.

22 The deed has passed, the monuments remain. (Motto of London Numismatic Society, taken from Ovid, *Fast.* 4.709)

23 Fortune has presented all the rewards to the victors. (Sallust, *Cat.* 20)

24 Drunkenness, through which all honor is lost, is no good. (Med.)

25 Truth hates delays. (Seneca, *Oed.* 871)
> If a person knows the truth about something, he should hurry up and tell it.

26 Prosperity has made me poor. (Ovid, *M.* 3.466)
> I have had so much that I have become greedy.

Poems

Catullus, you call me your heir.
Catullus, I won't believe it unless I read it. (Martial, 12.73)

> Hurry up and die, so I can read in the will that I am your heir and thus get the money.

> The construction of the first line is a form of indirect statement, with the verb *esse*. However, if the teacher tells the students that *dīcō* can take two accusatives ("you call me something"), this construction is near enough to English construction to offer no difficulty.

She never made any mistake, except the fact that she is dead. (Grave inscription)

The following poems are probably too difficult for the average high school class.

Zoilus is sick: his coverlets caused this fever./If he were well, what good would the scarlet covers do him?/What good this mattress from the Nile, dyed with the Sidonian dye of strong odor?/What does his sickness show except his stupid wealth?/ What do you need with doctors? Send away all your doctors./ Do you want to become well? Take *my* blankets. (Martial, 2.16)

> The dye used to dye clothes and blankets scarlet (the so-called imperial purple) was enormously expensive.

> Machaon was a physician in the *Iliad* and is here taken as a representative of all doctors. There are two constructions which the students have not had: *dīmitte* and *sūme* are imperatives, and *fierī* is the infinitive of the irregular verb *fīō*. The point of the poem is that Zoilus is just pretending to be sick in order to show off his fancy new bedclothes.

By chance I was asking for a loan of twenty thousand sesterces,/ which wouldn't have been a burdensome gift even if he'd *given* it to me./As a matter of fact, the person who was asked was a

rich and old friend of mine/and one whose money box has to
punish the riches which are overflowing in order to keep them
inside./He said to me, "You will be rich, if you plead law
cases."/Gaius, give me what I ask for: I don't ask for advice.
(Martial, 2.30)

> *Mūtuus* means "on loan" and is an adjective modifying
> *sestertia.*
>
> In line 2, instead of the subjunctive, Martial has chosen to
> use the indicative, thus making it more emphatic. However,
> it seems misleading in English to say "which was," and
> therefore "would" is used. *Fēlīx* here means "prosperous."
> In line 4, the figure is that of a money chest that has to
> whip the money (which is flowing around, *laxās*) in order
> to keep it within bounds. The students are told that the
> construction they have not had is the imperative *dā.* In
> line 6, *peto* is a poetic variant of *petō.* The person ad-
> dressed in line 6 is the old friend who wouldn't lend
> Martial the money.

Wherever you meet me, Postumus, you shout out/right away,
and this is your first word: "What are you doing?"/If you
meet me ten times in one hour,/you say this. I think, Postumus,
that you have nothing to do. (Martial, 2.67)

> The play in the poem is the contrast between *quid agis* and
> *quod agās. Quid agis* is the equivalent of "What are you
> doing?" and *Nīl quod agās* is the equivalent of "There is
> nothing which you could do if you had it to do." This is a
> nice contrast between the moods of indicative and sub-
> junctive, and will prepare the students for the structure
> when it is introduced to them.

Two praetors, four tribunes,
seven lawyers, ten poets
were asking for the hand of a certain young lady recently
from a certain older man. Without delay he
gave the girl to Eulogus, the auctioneer.
Tell me, Severus, he didn't act stupidly, did he? (Martial, 6.8)

> Auctioneers, executioners, and undertakers were outcasts
> in Roman society, since they presided over unpleasant

179

portions of life. The auctioneers seem to have made money, if we can believe Martial. Martial is saying that his contemporaries are so crazy about money that they would be willing to marry their daughter to an auctioneer.

The students are told that *morātus* is a participle of a deponent verb (although the term "deponent verb" is not used), and that *dīc* is the commanding form of the verb.

Word Game

It bites everything with its beak. (Anon.)

This is an acrostic. What bites with its beak is spelled out by the initial letters, *MORS*, or "death."

Additional Readings

Omnia perdidimus; tantum modo vīta relicta est.
We have lost all; only life is left. (Ovid, *Ex. P.* 4.16.49)

Plangere post factum mulieribus est satis aptum.
Weeping after the deed is suitable enough for women. (Med.)

Malus bonum ad sē numquam cōnsilium refert.
The evil person never applies good advice to himself. (Publilius Syrus)

Dulcia nōn meminit quī nōn gustāvit amāra.
Who has not tasted bitter things does not remember things that are sweet. (Med.)

No one can appreciate good fortune who has not experienced bad.

Quī scēptra saevus dūrō imperiō regit, timet timentēs.
Who savagely wields the scepter with harsh rule, fears those who are fearful. (Sir Philip Sidney, *Apology for Poetry?*)

Harsh government causes fear among those who rule as well as those who are ruled.

Gravis est inimīcus is quī latet in pectore.
The enemy which hides in our hearts is dangerous. (Publilius Syrus)

A person can be his own worst enemy.

UNIT 30

Story

I am indebted for this story to the late Professor Warren E. Blake. We have expanded the original story with details about food and dining in order to reinforce the filmstrips, *Vīta Cottīdiāna* and *Duo Amīcī*.

"The Ship"

In a certain city there was a house which was called "The Ship" by everyone. An amusing story is often told about this name.

In this city there was a young man who was very fond of banquets. One day he invited his friends to a large dinner. He himself went with his slaves to the market where he bought food.

Late in the day his friends came to dinner, and reclined at the table. First were brought in the appetizers: oysters, lettuce, bread, eggs, along with sweet wine. This wine, however, was mixed with water. After they had eaten enough of the appetizers, other courses were brought in: meat, fish, chicken, vegetables such as carrots and beets. Now water was no longer mixed in the wine; it was drunk undiluted. The carefree young men told jokes in loud voices.

The last course consisted of sweets and nuts. Finally one of the guests climbed on a table and tried to dance. But in vain. He fell to the floor.

The other guests laughed at him. "You're drunk!" they cried. He denied this, "I'm not drunk! I'm v-v-v-very sober. The table moved, and for this reason I fell."

Everyone was convulsed with laughter. "Stupid! How does the table move?" they said. "On board ship, it's true, tables often move. But we're on land, not at sea."

182

He seized one of the servants. "Where are we?" he asked. "Aren't we on board ship?"

"Yes," replied the terrified slave, "as you say, master, we're on board ship."

"Aha!" he exclaimed. "Go to the devil, table!" Saying this, he shoved the innocent table violently with his foot. This blow propelled the table against another friend. "Look!" said the latter. "The table moved against me. In truth, we are in a ship and not in a building! A great storm is attacking us! We are in terrible danger! Bring help to the ship! Throw everything into the sea! In this way we can save our lives!"

With loud shouts the young men started to throw everything out the window—tables, couches, and boxes. The frightened slaves did not dare to try to stop them. By accident somebody overturned a jar, from which water flowed out onto the floor. A young man saw this water flowing on the floor. "Oh, dear!" he cried. "Now our ship is sinking! Leave the sinking ship!" He tried to make his way through a window, where he stuck, shouting loudly. Hearing his shouts, a large crowd gathered in front of the building. The neighbors finally summoned the police, who led the weeping young men off to jail.

On the next day they were called to court. Their heads were aching from an excess of wine. The judge, serious and stern, asked, "Why did you raise such a rumpus? You have aroused honest citizens from their sleep. Why did you do this?"

"We were trying to save our lives in that great storm," said one of them.

The angry judge said, "You are crazy! There was no storm!"

"Oh, yes, there was!" replied the other. "There was an enormous storm. Look! Because of this storm even now we're all seasick!"

183

Questions

1 Quid est locus ubī cibum juvenis ēmit? Macellum.
2 Quae genera cibōrum ēmit juvenis? Ostreās, lactūcam,
pānem, ōva, vīnum, carnem, piscēs, pullōs, holera, carōtās,
bētās, dulcia, nucēs.
3 Ē quibus cōnstitit ferculum ultimum? Ē dulcibus et nucibus.
4 Quāliter juvenēs jocōs nārrābant? Hilariter.
5 Quō locō quīdam saltāre temptāvit? In mēnsā.
6 Ē quō dēfluit aqua in pavīmentum? Ex urnā.
7 Quō locō haesit juvenis territus? In fenestrā.
8 Ā quibus vocātī sunt custōdēs? Ā vīcīnīs.
9 Quō locō dormīvērunt juvenēs? In carcere.
10 Quālī sub jūdice erant? Sevērō gravīque.
11 Quid rē vērā juvenēs aegrōs fēcerat? Vīnum.

Readings

1 Who lives a life run by doctors, lives an unhappy life.
(Anon.)
Here the literal translation, "Who lives medically, lives
unhappily," certainly must be recast.

2 The lyre player is laughed at who always makes a mistake
on the same string. (Horace, *A.P.* 355-6)

3 He sins twice who denies his crime. (Anon.)

4 Who tries to please everybody labors in vain. (Anon.)

5 We do not usually believe an untruthful man, even when he
is telling the truth. (Cicero, *De Divin.* 2.146)

6 If Fortune wants, you will become a consul from being a
rhetorician;/and if the same Fortune wishes, you will become
a rhetorician from being a consul. (Juvenal, 7.197-8)
It is necessary for the students to realize that the upper
class of Romans did not work at any profession except
politics, and that although they might send their sons to a

rhetorician for training, they would not consider this a proper profession for him.

7 Lofty Corinth was not built in a single day. (Anon.)
The modern saying is that Rome was not built in a day.

8 The person who does not have any other gifts gives pears and fruit. (Med.)

9 Each person is the creator of his own fortune. (Appius Claudius Caecus)
There are variant forms of this quotation. The source is the *Epistula ad Caesarem*, sometimes called *De Republica Ordinanda*, whose authorship has been attributed by some to Sallust. The full quotation is *"In carminibus Appius ait fabrum esse quemque fortūnae."*

10 There are as many sorrows in love as there are shells on the seashore. (Ovid, *A.A.* 2.519)

11 Our bodies grow slowly but perish quickly. (Tacitus, *Agr.* 3)

12 Among the blind the one-eyed rules. (Anon.)

13 Fortune never stands in the same place;/she always moves; she changes and varies her ways,/and turns the highest into low and raises up what has been overthrown. (Ausonius, *Epigr.* 143.1)

14 Who is always afraid is condemned every day. (Anon.)

15 The burden which is carried well becomes light. (Anon.)

16 Happy is he who owes nothing. (Anon.)

17 Whoever has money sails with a safe breeze. (Petronius, 137)

18 Who loves well, chastises well. (Evidently a reflection of the passage from *Hebrews* 12.6: *Quem . . . dīligit Deus castīgat.*)

185

19 As the king is, so are the common people. (Burton)

20 Not everything which shines is gold. (Anon.)

21 He is a friend who in a difficult situation assists you with material help. (Plautus, *Epid.* 113)

22 The thorn which, when touched, produces pain, bears the flower. (Anon.)

23 Poverty is not something which possesses few things but which does not possess many things. (Seneca, *Ep.* 87.39)
    It is the *desire* for material possessions which makes a man poor.

24 With a grain of salt. (Anon.)

25 The voice of one crying in the desert. (*Matthew* 3.3)

26 Behold the Lamb of God, who takes away the sins of the world. (*I John* 29)

27 A bad end to a bad beginning. (Anon.)

28 Rashness hides under the name of bravery. (Seneca, *Ep.* 45.6)

29 People commit the same crime with different results;/one person gets the cross (crucifixion) as a reward for his evil, the other person gets a crown. (Juvenal, 13.10-5)

30 The effect of a liberal education is great. (Cicero, *Pro Rosc.* 63)

31 Honor is the reward for virtue. (Motto)

32 From Africa there is always something new. (Pliny the Elder, *N.H.* 8.17, adapted)
    Novī is a genitive modifying the pronoun *aliquid*. As so often, the common quotation does not use the exact words of the author. Pliny used indirect statement and said:

Vulgāre Graeciae dictum semper aliquid novī Āfricam afferre. ("There is a common Greek proverb which says 'Africa always offers something new.'")

33 The forehead (face) is the doorway to the mind. (Quintus Cicero)

34 The eye is not any good which does not see anything. (Med.)
Nīl is an adverbial accusative with the verb *prōdest.*

35 The shadow of a great name remains. (Lucan, *Phar.* 1.135, said of Pompey)
He has only his reputation left.

Poems

The shrewd thief will break open the money chest and take away your money;/the impious fire will lay low your ancestral Lares;/your debtor will deny both the interest and the principal;/the sterile field will not give back the seed which has been thrown on it (you won't even reap as much harvest as the amount of seed you put on it);/a deceptive girl friend will cheat your paymaster;/the ocean wave will destroy the ships loaded with merchandise./Whatever is given to friends is outside the grasp of fortune;/the only riches you will have forever are the ones which you have given away. (Martial, 5.42)

> This poem contains a number of new words. The problem is to get the student to see the structure. The good student will note that the first six lines all contain a verb in the future tense; obviously these are all parallel circumstances. Once a student starts on the series, it becomes much easier for him to decipher the meaning. There are no structures here which the students have not had.

> The *Larēs* were the household gods, themselves formerly human beings, who stayed around the house to help the present owners. There is a variant form *Lārēs*, with /ā/ in the first syllable.

The first and second hours wear out those making the morning salutation;/the third hour exercises the hoarse lawyers;/Rome extends various labors into the fifth hour;/the sixth hour is a siesta for those who are tired; the seventh hour will be its completion;/the eighth hour stretches into the ninth hour in the shining gymnasium;/the ninth hour orders us to crush the bolsters which have been arranged for us (at dinner);/the tenth hour is the one for my books, Euphemus,/when your attention arranges the ambrosial feast/and noble Caesar is relaxed with heavenly nectar/and holds tiny cups in his mighty hand./Then let in the jokes: do you go with wanton step,/ Thalia, to Jupiter in the morning? (Martial, 4.8)

Notice how many times Martial says that Domitian is a god. One might be tempted to think that Martial was a sincere admirer of the Emperor, who was so unpopular with others, if it were not for the fact that after Domitian's death, Martial did not hesitate to criticize him. For example, in a poem written after Domitian had died, he says that in spite of the fact that the first two members of the Flavian family (Vespasian and Titus) were so good, the third (Domitian) was so poor that he almost outweighed the two good ones:

Flāvia gēns, quantum tibi tertius abstulit hērēs!
    Paene fuit tantī nōn habuisse duōs. (*Ep.* 33)

O Flavian family! How much honor the third descendant has robbed you of./It almost would have been better not to have had the two good ones (Vespasian and Titus)!

Before the students proceed to look up individual words, they ought to be able to see that the poem describes how the first ten hours of the Roman day are spent. Since Domitian demanded he be called *Dominus et Deus*, the teacher should have the students discover how many times Domitian is referred to as divine (his feast is ambrosial, he drinks heavenly nectar, and he is actually called Jupiter).

The students have been told that *admitte* is the commanding form of the verb, that -*n* on *gressūn* is a variant of -*ne*, and that *mētīre* is a deponent verb in the second person meaning "to measure" or "to walk." They have also learned that the gymnasium is called "shining" for several reasons (athletes shone from rubbing oil; baths were marble), and that the phrase "crushing the bolsters" means lying down on carefully arranged couches.

Here are a few other details which might help them. Domitian is too busy to read Martial's poems during the day, but will read them after supper. Euphemus is the steward in charge of meals. *Matutīnum* is an adjective modifying *Jovem*, and meaning "morning."

In spite of all of Martial's efforts, the biographer Suetonius tells us that Domitian cared nothing for poetry.

You will dine well, my Fabullus, at my house/in a few days, if the gods favor you,/if you bring with you a good, big/dinner along with a pretty girl/and wine and salt-and-wit and all kinds of laughter./If you bring these things with you, I say, my charming friend/you will dine well./For the purse of your friend Catullus is full of spiderwebs./But in return you will get unadulterated affection/or anything which is more pleasant or lovelier than that./For I will give you an ointment which/ the Venuses and Cupids gave my girl,/which when you smell it, you will ask the gods,/Fabullus, to make you all nose. (Catullus, 13)

> In line 5 in the translation, we have tried to reproduce the double meaning of *sale* as "salt" and "wit." The students have had explained to them the new form *suāvius* and *ēlegantius* which are comparative forms of the neuter. They have also had explained to them that a demand is made with *rogō, ut,* and the subjunctive.

I admit, you gave a fine ointment
to your guests yesterday, but you didn't cut any meat.
It's a funny thing to smell good, and go hungry.
Who does not dine and is anointed with ointment, Fabullus,
he seems to me to really be a dead person. (Martial, 3.12)

> While Martial's poem is understandable in its own right, its humor really lies in its reference to the Catullus poem which we have included above.

> *Fateor* is a deponent verb. *Here* is a variant for *herī.*

189

Hey, there, that's enough, little book;/we have now come right down to the end (the rod on which the papyrus was rolled)./ But you want to proceed further and go on,/and you can't be held in on this last strip of papyrus,/just as if your business were not already done,/which was really already done on the first page./And now the reader complains and stops reading,/ and now the copyist says this too,/"Hey, there, little book, that's enough!" (Martial, 4.89)

The new constructions are the passive infinitive *tenērī* in line 4, the subjunctive in line 5, and the deponent verb *queritur* in line 7.

Martial is talking to his book as though it were a living person who wants to go on and on, much to everyone's disgust. Martial says, "Your job is done; as a matter of fact, your job was done on the first page, as one page of epigrams is enough." Martial frequently observed that a whole book of epigrams was too much to digest at one time.

Additional Readings

Beātī oculī quī tē vīdērunt.
Blessed are the eyes which have beheld thee. (Anon.)

Semel īnsānīvimus omnēs.
We have all been unwise on one occasion. (Anon.)

Meminērunt omnia amantēs.
Lovers remember everything. (Ovid, *Her.* 15.43)

Bēstia crūdēlis est cor prāvae mulieris.
The heart of a wicked woman is a cruel beast. (Med.)

In mōrēs nōn habet fortūna jūs.
Fortune does not have jurisdiction over human character. (Seneca, *Ep.* 36.6)
Bad luck should not change your character.

Artes Latinae
on
CD-ROM

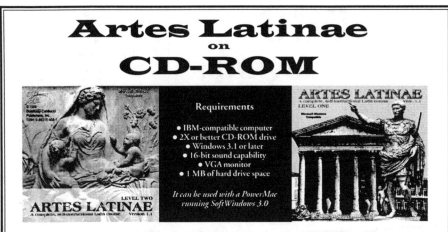

Requirements

- IBM-compatible computer
- 2X or better CD-ROM drive
- Windows 3.1 or later
- 16-bit sound capability
- VGA monitor
- 1 MB of hard drive space

It can be used with a PowerMac running SoftWindows 3.0

To give students the advantage of modern technology,
Bolchazy-Carducci Publishers, Inc. has produced a

CD-ROM version of *Artes Latinae.*

Based on the original edition created by Dr. Waldo E. Sweet, *et alii,* this edition has been developed through the efforts of Dr. Jeffrey Lyon and Dr. Robert P. Sonkowsky.

Each disk contains text, illustrations, and sound. A manual to the program accompanies the disk. Reference notebooks, tests and test guides, and graded readers must be purchased separately.

Pronunciation options on CD-ROM

- *American Scholastic.* This is a classical pronunciation recorded by Dr. Waldo E. Sweet.

- *Restored Classical.* Today we have sufficient evidence of the sounds of Classical Latin to be able to pronounce those sounds with a high degree of accuracy. Robert Sonkowsky has assimilated these restored sounds into his readings. These sounds do not differ to a great extent from the American scholastic pronunciation. The most salient difference is the treatment of the word-final "m" as a sign of nasalization of the preceding vowel.

- *Continental Ecclesiastical.* This pronunciation is most appropriately used with Medieval and Neo-Latin materials.

Check out our website for more information
Download a demo
(http://www.bolchazy.com/al/alcddemo.html)

Bolchazy-Carducci Publishers, Inc.
1000 Brown St., Unit 101, Wauconda, IL 60084 USA; *Phone:* 847/526-4344; *Fax:* 847/526-2867
E-mail: latin@bolchazy.com; *Website:* http://www.bolchazy.com

Traditional Format

ARTES LATINAE

By Waldo E. Sweet

Published by Bolchazy-Carducci Publishers, Inc.

1000 Brown Street, Unit 101, Wauconda, IL 60084 (800) 392-6453, **www.bolchazy.com**

Originally published by Encyclopædia Britannica

LEVEL I-- in Four Phases

Phase	QTY	Materials/Descriptions	Order #	Unit Price	Total
Phase I ___ #0101	___ ___ ___ ___	Student Text, Book I[1] Unit Test Booklet (consumable*) Reference Notebook (consumable*) Guide to Unit Tests Three Audio Cassette Tapes ($14.00 each) (units 1-2: #359-6, 3-4: #360-X, 5-6: #361-8)	290-5 293-X 295-6 298-0	___ ___ ___ ___
Phase II ___ #0102	___ ___ ___	Graded Reader (Lectiones Primae) TM Graded Reader Teachers Manual Four Audio Cassette Tapes ($14.00 each) (units 7-8: #362-6, 9-10: #363-4, 11-12: #364-2, 13-14: #365-0)	294-8 297-2 296-4	___ ___ ___
Phase III ___ #0103	___ ___	Student Text Book II Four Audio Cassette Tapes ($14.00 each) (units 15-16: #366-9, 17-18: #367-7, 19-20: #368-5, 21-22: #369-3)	292-1	___
Phase IV ___ #0104	___	Four Audio Cassettes Tapes ($14.00 each) (units 23-24: #370-7, 25-26: #371-5, 27-28: #372-3, 29-30: 373-1)		___
___		Complete Level I Package (SAVE $43.00)	393-6	___

LEVEL II-- in Four Phases

Phase	QTY	Materials/Descriptions	Order #	Unit Price	Total
Phase I ___ #0201	___ ___ ___ ___ ___	Student Text, Book I Unit Test Booklet (consumable*) Guide to Unit Tests Reference Notebook (consumable*) Teacher's Manual Two Audio Cassette Tapes ($14.00 each) (units 1-2: #375-8, 3-4: #376-6)	299-9 301-4 306-5 303-0 304-9	___ ___ ___ ___ ___
Phase II ___ #0202	___ ___	Graded Reader (Lectiones Secundae) TM Graded Reader Four Audio Cassette Tapes ($14.00 each) (units 5-6: #377-4, 7-8: #378-2, 9-10: #379-0, 11-12: #380-4)	234-4 305-7	___ ___
Phase III ___ #0203	___	Student Text, Book II Three Audio Cassette Tapes ($14.00 each) (units 13-14: #382-0, 15-16: #383-9, 17-18: #384-7)	300-6	___
Phase IV ___ #0204	___	Three Audio Cassette Tapes ($14.00 each) (units 19-20: #385-5, 21-22: #386-3, 23-24: #387-1)		___
___		Complete Level II Package (SAVE $24)	394-4	___

* Purchase additional Reference Notebooks and Unit Test Booklets for each student!

***** **Please fill out customer mailing and credit card information on the other side.** *****